MO[...]

SCOTT GAMM is the founder of HelpSaveMyDollars.com, a financial website focused on helping consumers save money. He has appeared on NBC's *Today* show, CNBC's *Closing Bell*, MSNBC, CNN, *Inside Edition*, Fox Business Network, ABC News, and CBS.

He is a writer for CNBC.com, *Forbes*, and TheStreet.com, and a contributor to *The Huffington Post* and Business Insider.com.

Scott has contributed to articles for FoxBusiness.com, the Associated Press, Reuters, *Family Circle*, *USA Today*, *Woman's World* magazine, and others.

Scott studies finance, marketing, and communications at New York University Stern School of Business.

Praise for *More Money, Please*

"Gamm demystifies everything from credit scores to student loans in an easy-to-understand and entertaining way. Highly recommended!"
—Stephanie Nelson, *New York Times* bestselling author of *The Coupon Mom's Guide to Cutting Your Grocery Bills in Half*

"*More Money, Please* sheds light on the financial woes that have plagued young people for decades. If you're ready to get your financial house in order, read Scott Gamm's book!"
—William D. Cohan, *New York Times* bestselling author of *Money and Power: How Goldman Sachs Came to Rule the World*

"*More Money, Please* is the go-to source for smart and simple answers to the most pressing financial issues facing young people. An excellent read!"
—Jean Chatzky, financial [...]

D0390872

MORE MONEY, PLEASE

The Financial Secrets You
Never Learned in School

SCOTT GAMM

A PLUME BOOK

PLUME
Published by the Penguin Group
Penguin Group (USA) Inc., 375 Hudson Street,
New York, New York 10014, USA

USA | Canada | UK | Ireland | Australia
New Zealand | India |South Africa | China
Penguin Books Ltd, Registered Offices: 80 Strand, London WC2R 0RL, England
For more information about the Penguin Group visit penguin.com

First published by Plume, a member of Penguin Group (USA) Inc., 2013

 REGISTERED TRADEMARK—MARCA REGISTRADA

LIBRARY OF CONGRESS CATALOGING-IN-PUBLICATION DATA
Gamm, Scott.
   More money, please : the financial secrets you never learned in school /
Scott Gamm.
      pages cm
   "A Plume book."
   Includes bibliographical references and index.
   ISBN 978-0-452-29843-9 (pbk.)
1. Finance, Personal. 2. High school graduates—Finance, Personal. 3. College
students—Finance, Personal. I. Title.
   HG179.G272 2013
   332.024—dc23   2012049212

Printed in the United States of America
10   9   8   7   6   5   4   3   2   1

Set in Janson LT Std.
Designed by Eve L. Kirch

PUBLISHER'S NOTE
This publication is designed to provide accurate and authoritative information in regard
to the subject matter covered. It is sold with the understanding that the publisher is not
engaged in rendering legal, accounting, or other professional services. If you require
legal advice or other expert assistance, you should seek the services of a competent
professional.

While the author has made every effort to provide accurate telephone numbers, Internet
addresses, and other contact information at the time of publication, neither the publisher
nor the author assumes any responsibility for errors or for changes that occur after
publication. Further, publisher does not have any control over and does not assume any
responsibility for author or third-party Web sites or their content.

To my parents, Donna and Harvey,
and my sisters, Shari and Lindsay

Contents

Introduction: My Story

They say money makes the world go round, but what happens when it turns your life upside down?

When I was a kid, life was good. I grew up in a middle-class town on Long Island, with loving parents and two older sisters whom I admired and looked up to. My family went on vacations and frequently ate out at restaurants; we were always laughing and having a good time together, no matter what we did. But the family dynamic changed when the recession hit. Bills started piling up, and that led to a lot of tension in the house. My parents' arguments seemed never-ending, and eventually the financial stress was just too much. They divorced when I was fifteen. My world was rocked. It just didn't seem possible: how could money cause such pain?

From that point on, I promised myself that I would learn everything I could about money, to make *sure* the financial headaches of my childhood wouldn't repeat themselves later on in adulthood. But there was a problem: easy-to-understand information about money didn't exist for people my age.

Because I was kind of a nerd, I went into research overdrive. I read dozens of personal finance books for adults and watched financial TV shows, trying to make sense of how to be successful. Did I need to play the stock market? Did I have to have a trust fund? I saw example after example that proved one doesn't *need* any of those things to be financially savvy. It seemed that with a little bit of work, determination, and tenacity anybody could make smart financial decisions and live a life full of security.

When I talked to friends whose families had also experienced hardship in the economic downturn, I realized I wasn't alone in my concern about finances. We were all anxious about, and worried and overwhelmed by, money. I wanted to share what I had learned, so I decided to write up all the information I had gathered in my quest to conquer my personal finances and put it into a website. I started HelpSaveMyDollars.com in 2009, and the reaction has been overwhelming. Nothing excites me more than getting e-mails from readers who have benefited from the info on the site. The message is clear: our generation isn't going to stand idly by and watch our personal finances wreak havoc on our lives. We want to be in control of our money, and, hell, let's be honest: we want *more* of it.

As I wrap up my junior year of college at New York University's Stern School of Business, news about the economy is still shaky at best, and it doesn't look like it's going to get better anytime soon. I understand how tough it is for people my age to start out on the right financial footing. And that's why I decided to write this book: so people like me would have a source they could relate to for information about money. I don't want to be preached at or talked down to. I just want practical knowledge that's easy to implement. And that's what I hope to offer here. What's the point of reading a finance book if the info is too dense to be put into action?

How This Book Will Help

When it comes to money, the statistics for my generation are downright scary. Consider these figures:

1. Outstanding student loan debt now stands at $1 trillion, according to the Consumer Financial Protection Bureau.[1]

2. The average student has over $3,100 of credit card debt.[2]

3. Only 17 percent of students pay off their credit card bill every month.[3]

4. The average student has five credit cards.[4]

Since we all have to deal with money at some point in our lives—no matter what job or field we work in—you might think money management classes would be mandatory in high schools and colleges. Nope! Only four states require students to take a stand-alone personal finance class in high school: Virginia, Utah, Tennessee, and Missouri.[5] This means the majority of us head off to college without any financial training. And it's not our fault! I'm a *business* major, and when I talk to my academic advisers about what courses

I'm required to take at the college level, personal finance isn't one of them!

But just because your education didn't prepare you doesn't mean you can't acquire the knowledge you need now. And that's where this book comes in. Think of it as the personal finance class that never existed in school—without the homework and tests.

I'm going to walk you step-by-step through every money-related topic you'll need to understand, including the following:

1. How to save money easily, regardless of your income
2. How to pick a bank that cares about you (yes, it is possible!)
3. How to conquer your student loan debt
4. How Twitter and LinkedIn can help you land an internship or a job
5. How to accumulate almost $300,000 in retirement savings with just $33 a month

But before we start, what financial goals do you want to achieve? We all have aspirations and ideas about what we would like to do with our money—whether it's paying down debt, saving for a vacation, or being able to buy a home one day. When the going gets tough, it's important to remember these goals. Your goals are your lifeboat, your motivation, your reason for picking up this book.

Go ahead, write down three money-related goals:

1 _____
2. _____
3. _____

And, hey, just because I'm writing a personal finance book doesn't mean I've achieved all my goals. Here are three of my financial aspirations:

1. To save at least 10 percent of my income and have enough left over for one vacation a year
2. To be debt-free at *all* times
3. To have robust retirement savings, without the government's help

You and I will be on track to achieve our goals by the end of this book, I promise. What are you waiting for? Let's get started!

MORE
MONEY,
PLEASE

1

TAKE THE BORE OUT
OF BUDGETING

When you hear the word "budgeting," you probably think of calculators, paperwork, formulas, and time that could be better spent hanging out with friends, lying on the beach, or watching movies on Netflix. I'm going to let you in on a secret: budgeting isn't nearly as miserable as you might imagine. Now, I'm not going to try to convince you that it is the most *exciting* thing in the world (even if I am a numbers guy), but it definitely doesn't have to be a painful, difficult, or time-consuming task. Forget the idea that only soccer moms or guys in suits need to create budgets, because creating a budget is one of *the* most important things you can do to be financially successful in the long run. The hour or so it'll take each month will be one of the most worthwhile hours you spend in front of a computer—I promise.

Managing your financial life without a budget is like driving a car with a blindfold on. A budget forces you to look at the big picture: how much you earn, how much you spend and where, and how much you save. If you want more money in

your pocket—and that's why you're reading this book, right?—
you need to figure out exactly where it's going every month.

Consider the items you buy without even thinking: mag-
azines, a box of tissues when you're sick, gum, apps for your
phone. These are what I like to call "budget killers." You need
to become conscious of these types of purchases if you want
to take control of your financial life. Budgets aren't made by
guesstimating, so I'm going to ask you to look honestly at
how you spend your money, down to the penny.

After creating a budget, you'll know exactly what expenses
need to be reduced in your life. Let's say you're the type of person who buys coffee every day of the week. Chances are, you
probably don't even think twice about getting in line at Starbucks for your morning java fix! Once you start tracking your
spending, though, you'll immediately become aware of how
much of your hard-earned money is going toward your caffeine
habit. Armed with that knowledge, you can start to change your
behavior—maybe choosing to buy coffee three days a week instead of seven. Little changes like this will free up money for the
things you *really* want in life, whether that means building up
your savings account, paying down student loan debt, buying a
new computer, or saving toward a trip to Europe. I'd take any of
those things over a Venti Latte—wouldn't you? This doesn't
mean you need to completely stop buying coffee!

Determining How Much You Make

So I hope I have you convinced: you have to make a budget.
Now, how do you actually do it? Trust me. It's *not* that bad.

The first step in making a budget is to determine how much money you make in a given month, after taxes have been paid. You may have a fixed yearly salary, your income may fluctuate due to commissions or bonuses, or you may have an hourly wage—it doesn't matter how you earn your money as long as you can account for it.

A Tax "Break"

Believe it or not, taxes may be one of your largest expenses. The not-for-profit Tax Foundation estimates that we paid some $4 trillion in taxes in 2012—$152 billion more than we spent on food, housing, and clothing. Additionally, our country worked some 107 days just to pay our tax bills (federal, state, and local).[1]

The best way to determine how much you make in a month is to look at your pay stubs, which will tell you how much money was removed from your paycheck and directed to the government. Assuming you get paid biweekly (that's two paychecks per month), just add up the after-tax amounts shown on each of your pay stubs for that particular month. That is the number you should use for your budget, okay?

Tracking Each Penny

Now that you know how much you make each month, how do you figure out how much you spend?

Your larger expenses—like rent, car payment, and cell phone bill—should stay the same each month. But smaller expenditures—for things like groceries, dry cleaning, or going to movies, bars, or restaurants—vary from month to month. Those are the ones you have to watch out for. They're the budget killers, and you need to account for them down to the penny. Read that again: *down to the penny*. But don't worry—tracking your expenses is easy, I promise.

Here are three simple ways to do it:

1. Keep Your Receipts: Every time you make a purchase stick the receipt in your wallet, and then throw it in a shoe box or a drawer when you get home. At the end of every month take an hour and tally up all the receipts and categorize the expenditures (more on this in a minute).

This is an effective yet old-fashioned way to track the money you spend. I'm not a big fan of this method. I've tried it, but keeping all your receipts requires a ton of self-discipline. This approach is best if you're very anal and organized (you know who you are!).

2. Use Your Debit or Credit Card Statements: If you use a debit card or credit card to make purchases, a list of your expenditures will be sent to you in the mail or will be made accessible online via your monthly statements. It's so easy to track them this way. The statement adds up all the purchases made over a thirty-day period, so you don't even have to pull out a calculator. All the work is done for you.

A word to the wise: don't rely on a credit card unless you have the cash on hand to back up each purchase.

You'll get into debt if you can't pay off the balance in full each month, which is something we all want to avoid. We'll get into this in more detail in chapter 6.

3. Use Your Smartphone: The third and most tech-savvy way to track your spending is to use an app on your smartphone. The free iPhone and Android app ABUKAI allows users to take a picture of their receipt after making a purchase in a store. The app stores this data, allowing you to easily track your spending and tally up your expenditures. Crazy simple, right?

It doesn't matter which of these methods you use—in fact, you might use a combination of the three, especially if you're going back and forth between using cash and a card. As long as you're consistent about tracking your spending, you'll be able to create a budget without a problem.

How to Create a Budget

All right, so now that you've determined how much you earn, and you've got your expenses stored either physically or electronically, you're ready to create your budget. Let's do it!

To start, open up an Excel file and create a heading that displays your monthly earnings after taxes. Next you're going to subtract *all* your expenses from your monthly earnings. To do this, list each type of expense separately. Be as specific as possible—don't just lump together everything you spent at the mall, movies, and restaurants into one category. The more exact you are, the easier it'll be for you to see where you can cut back on unnecessary expenses. Let's look at an example together. Here's the budget of twenty-three-year-old Jonathan, a single guy living in New York City:

Income	
Monthly income	$2,740

Expenses	
Rent	$900
Cell phone	$50
Groceries	$300
Cable TV/Internet	$105
Utilities	$98
Commuting costs	$174
Clothing	$246.38
Dry cleaning	$31.23
Gym membership	$97
Restaurants	$280
Bars	$220.73
Froyo	$20
Coffee	$98.41
Medicine	$41
Magazines	$6
Dermatologist copay	$40
Total Expenses:	**$2,707.75**
Savings:	**$32.25**

Note how specific the budget is. Jonathan may not even remember buying those strawberry Froyos a few weeks ago, but he spent money on them, so they have to be included in the budget.

So is Jonathan in good shape? Sort of. Hopefully after you deduct your expenses from your income, you'll have some money left over too. If you don't, that means you have a deficit—that is, you are spending more than you earn. Jonathan is saving about $32 a month, which isn't great, but it's certainly better than a deficit. Now that we've got the full picture of what Jonathan's spending looks like, it's time to figure out where his expenses can be reduced so he's not left with such a paltry sum.

Here's what his budget would look like if he cut his spending at restaurants by half and went to a cheaper gym:

Income	
Monthly income	$2,740
Expenses	
Rent	$900
Cell phone	$50
Groceries	$300
Cable TV/Internet	$105
Utilities	$98
Commuting costs	$174
Clothing	$246.38
Dry cleaning	$31.23
Gym membership	**$48.50**
Restaurants	**$140**
Bars	$220.73
Froyo	$20
Coffee	$98.41

(continued)

Medicine	$41
Magazines	$6
Dermatologist copay	$40
Total Expenses:	**$2,519.25**
Savings:	**$220.75**

Yes, he had to cut back on the dinner dates and try out a gym with equipment that isn't brand new, but look how much extra he is saving: $221 per month versus $32. That's more than *seven* times what he was saving with his old budget-free lifestyle.

Everyone's spending preferences vary. Let's say Jonathan's not the type of person who would want to cut his spending on restaurants in half. Think about other changes Jonathan might make to his budget. He could cut down on his shopping sprees at clothing stores or his daily treks to Starbucks. (Ever hear of the Keurig? It makes great coffee!) Or maybe Jonathan should consider moving to a cheaper area, outside New York City. You get the picture. It doesn't matter how you reduce your budget as long as you have money left over after all your expenses have been paid.

You might be thinking, hey, I understand that it's good to save, but is it worth making all these sacrifices just to have a few extra bucks? It *definitely* is. Think of it this way: Jonathan, like most Americans, could lose his job at any time. What if he walked into work tomorrow and found out his job was cut? How could he live his current lifestyle if he lost his job and income for a period of six months? Simply put—he couldn't. That's why he needs to work extra hard on his budget while he has a job and to put away money that could be used for unexpected emergencies. It's just smart thinking, no way around it.

To build your savings, you should aim to put aside 10 percent of your total income every month. That might seem like a lot, but I promise you it'll be worth it in the long run. You'll sleep easier knowing you have a cushion!

Saving Money with Your Eyes Closed

What if you could save money instantly, without even thinking about it? What if "saving money" was another expense on your budget?

This is what is known as "automating" your savings, or having a certain amount of money transferred from your checking account into your savings account each month. It forces you to make do with less while building up your savings at the same time. Pretty great system, right? It gets better, because setting up an automated transfer takes less than thirty seconds.

Simply log on to your online bank account and click on the Transfers tab. Here's what you should see on your screen:

Transfer From:	Checking account no. 2421
Transfer To:	Savings account no. 8241
Amount:	$275
Transfer Date:	April 1, 2013
Frequency:	Select one: one-time, weekly, twice per month, **monthly**, every four weeks, every two months, quarterly, every six months, yearly
Number of Transfers:	Fixed [choose a specific number] or **unlimited**

Jonathan would choose to transfer $275 a month, or 10 percent of his monthly take-home pay of $2,740. It'll be transferred from his checking account into his savings account every month (that's why he selected "monthly" in the Frequency section). He wants to do this indefinitely, so he would choose "unlimited" in the Number of Transfers section. Automatic transfers occur on the same day every month, which means you don't have to do anything but watch your savings account grow.

It's that easy! So you have no excuse not to do it.

Even if you automate your savings, you're not off the hook when it comes to keeping a monthly budget. In fact, automating your savings makes your monthly take-home pay smaller, so you're going to have to make other cuts in your spending to avoid running into a deficit.

Let's go back to the example of Jonathan's budget. He brings home $2,740 a month after taxes. Ten percent of that ($275) goes directly into his savings, leaving him just $2,465 to spend during the month. Here is what Jonathan's automatic-savings-adjusted budget will look like, keeping all other expenses the same:

Income	
Monthly income	$2,465
Expenses	
Rent	$900
Cell phone	$50
Groceries	$300
Cable TV/Internet	$105
Utilities	$98

Commuting costs	$174
Clothing	$246.38
Dry cleaning	$31.23
Gym membership	$48.50
Restaurants	$140
Bars	$220.73
Froyo	$20
Coffee	$98.41
Medicine	$41
Magazines	$6
Dermatologist copay	$40
Total Expenses:	**$2,519.25**
Savings:	**$–54.25**

Aha! A deficit of $54.25. It's not a true deficit (since $275 per month is automatically heading into his savings), but it's still a negative number on Jonathan's budget, and we don't want that!

See how powerful automated savings is? Not only are you guaranteed to save money, but because you're incorporating it into your budget, you're going to realize that you need to further reduce your expenses. Jonathan has to cut his expenses by an additional $54.25 if he's going to save 10 percent of his annual income and break even each month. A little less Froyo and a lot less clothes shopping would do the trick.

You cannot sustain a budget with a deficit. Being in the hole even as little as $54.25 a month adds up to $651 annually. We said a moment ago that Jonathan was saving 10 percent of his take-home income ($3,300 per year). Well, with a deficit of $651 he's really only saving $2,649 a year, which is not 10 percent of his income—it's about 8 percent. This may not sound like a huge difference, but when you have nothing in an emergency savings fund, that extra $651 might go a long way. It's time to get into gear and replace excuses with savings.

A Tip for Self-Discipline

How do you cut your spending? How do you resist the urge to spend? Here's one method I've found to be helpful.

Let's say your goal is to save up $5,000 toward a vacation in the Caribbean.

On the back of a business card, write "$5,000" in large print. Put this card in front of the credit and debit cards in your wallet, so when you try to take out your cards to make purchases, you have to remove the business card first. When you're out shopping and are tempted to buy that $150 pair of shoes (that you want but know you don't need), you'll be reminded of your goal as soon as you open your wallet. The shoes may not look so good after that. Frivolous purchases do nothing to move you closer to your goal of saving $5,000.

Over time, pursuing your financial goals will become so natural that you'll simply stop spending money on items you don't really need. And trust me: you'll love seeing your bank account grow.

Quick Review

Here's what you should remember from this chapter:

1. Figure out your specific short- and long-term financial goals and write them down!

2. Create a budget every month and track every penny you spend.

3. Automate your savings account so 10 percent of your monthly income goes into it.

4. If you find yourself in a deficit, then adjust your spending so you break even. It'll be worth it in the long run!

2

THE LAWS OF BANKING

I don't want to be the bearer of bad news, but our generation is getting screwed in a lot of ways. Whether it's the national debt approaching $17 trillion or the fact that there probably won't be enough Social Security money left by the time we retire, young people are getting it from all angles. And now banks are finding ways to mess with us too, with hidden fees and sneaky policies that hit us where it hurts the most: our wallets.

I remember my first experience with one of these fees. I was in high school and had just deposited a check from my part-time job into my checking account. When I looked online later, to make sure it had cleared, I noticed a charge that I didn't recognize, so I called up my bank's customer service line to report it. The rep told me that the charge wasn't an error—no, it was a fee *from the bank*. I was shocked. Here I was thinking that someone had stolen my card, when, really, my money was being "spent" by the people who were supposedly keeping it safe. The worst part was that the fee wasn't charged because I did anything wrong—I didn't overspend, or withdraw from a different bank's ATM—it was because I didn't have enough money in my account to meet the bank's minimum requirement. Of course I didn't— I was in high school, after all! I wasn't exactly rolling in dough.

Not only would the bank not waive the fee until I had at least $1,000 in the account, but I learned I had been paying this fee every month since I opened the account, six months before! Yes, $48 gone, just like that. It might not seem like much now, but for a high school kid that's about six hours worth of work down the drain.

Chances are you've had a similar, and similarly frustrating, experience. If you're not on your toes, banks will slam you with fees you don't even know exist.

Not every bank is an evil entity intent upon preying on its customers. But let's face it: banks are out there to earn a profit, just like any other business. It's up to you to make a smart decision when you pick a bank to use. So in this chapter we're going to cover the ins and outs of banking: how to find the best bank, how to avoid nasty fees, and how to navigate the world of debit cards.

Finding the Best Bank

If you already have a checking and savings account, cool beans! You're ahead of the game. That may not seem like a big deal, but, believe it or not, 17 million Americans don't have a bank account![1] If you're part of that group, you should stop putting your money in a piggy bank or under your mattress. You need both a checking account and a savings account. Period.

Why should you use a bank? Banks let you safely store your money, offering you security and stability. They can also lend you money if you need it for your college tuition or if you want to buy a car or house at some point in your life.

If you haven't been using a bank, or are dissatisfied with your current one, setting up an account is easy. You can choose one of the big banks (Bank of America, Chase), local banks in your area, or even credit unions, which are not-for-profit institutions. Before choosing one, make sure the bank is insured by the FDIC (Federal Deposit Insurance Corporation), which provides insurance up to $250,000 per account, so if the bank fails or closes down, you won't lose your money. Most banks are FDIC insured, so this shouldn't be a problem—it's just good to know.

Once you find out whether the bank is FDIC insured, go to your local branch and ask to speak with a representative who can help you open up checking and savings accounts (you'll need both). A checking account is where you deposit your money, either in check or cash form. They generally do not pay interest (although some online checking accounts from major banks do), since the account is simply for depositing and withdrawing money, rather than for building savings. A savings account, on the other hand, does pay interest but at a very minimal rate, usually 0.3–2 percent, depending on how the economy is doing. The interest rate is ultimately determined by the Federal Reserve (the government). The bank pays you interest, typically on a monthly basis (though some banks are different), as a reward for keeping your money in that bank.

All about Interest

If you walk by a bank and see a sign in the window advertising a 1 percent annual percentage rate (APR), this is the percentage it pays in interest, over the course of the year, on the money in your checking account. But the interest rate you *actually* receive is a bit different. The rate you earn is the effective annual rate (EAR), which takes into account compounding interest.

What's compounding interest? Compounding interest is interest built on interest. This is how it works: say you have $100 in a savings account with an annual interest rate of 1 percent. With that interest rate, you'll earn $1 in interest that year. The next year, due to compounding interest, you won't earn interest on the initial $100 but on $101 instead. The interest continues to build, paying not on the initial amount but on what you've accumulated in your savings from year to year. In the second year, your earnings from interest will be 1 percent of $101, which is $1.01, and so on and so on. Therefore the EAR is generally a bit higher than the APR, not high enough to get excited about, but good to know you have it nevertheless!

The representative will explain the bank's policies and ask you to provide some basic information for their records, like your photo ID, Social Security number, address, and phone number. Once that information is processed, the representative will give you account numbers for your checking and savings accounts. They'll be pretty long numbers that you probably won't remember. You'll need them when you want to deposit a check or withdraw funds from the bank (though not an ATM), so keep the numbers written down somewhere, but *not* in your wallet, because if you lose your wallet, well, someone will have your account number. The representative will also give you a checkbook, debit card, and information about the bank. Then you're ready to start banking with the rest of us. Easy, right?

Because of increased government regulation (notably the 2010 Dodd-Frank Act, which puts limits on the fees banks can charge), banks have been trying to find new ways to make money. You want to select a bank with the fewest fees (obviously!), but that's becoming harder to do these days. Just check out what megabank Wells Fargo is doing. In early 2012, it added a $7 monthly checking account fee for customers in select states, and it plans to extend the fee to all its customers.[2] Customers are charged $7 a month if they elect to have paper statements sent to them via mail or $5 for online statements. This is only waived with a minimum balance of $1,500.

And don't let out a sigh of relief because you're not a Wells Fargo customer. Bank of America has a similar monthly checking account fee on its MyAccess Checking account: $12 for those who maintain a balance below $1,500 or who don't make a direct deposit of at least $250 a month.

Here are some other crazy fees banks are charging:

1. **"ATM Not in Your Network" Fees:** Let's say you have a checking account at Chase. Need some money? Easy, just walk on into the nearest branch, withdraw what you need, and walk away without paying a fee. But let's say it's pouring rain, and the nearest Chase branch is ten blocks away, and you're feeling a little lazy. You *could* go to Chase, but there's a Citi branch right across the street from where you work. If you choose to use Citi's ATM to withdraw money, you'll be charged a fee of around $1.75 because your account is not at Citi. That's right—you're paying a fee just to withdraw your *own* money. In fact, just checking your balance at an ATM that's not a part of your bank's network could result in a fee (even if you don't end up taking out money). The lesson is use only your own bank's ATMs, even if you're feeling lazy.

2. **Minimum Daily Balance:** In addition to looking at your minimum monthly balance, some banks keep track of your minimum *daily* balance. At the end of each business day, if you don't have a certain amount in your account—say $200—the bank will charge you a fee. This doesn't mean your account can't ever dip below $200. If you make tons of purchases with your debit card one morning, and by mid-afternoon there's only $100 left in your account, you won't immediately be charged. As long as you make a deposit that brings your balance back above the minimum *before the bank closes* that day (in this case, you would need to deposit $100), you won't be charged a fee. But if you can't get to the bank, or

you don't have the money to meet the minimum, the bank can charge you. Tricky, right?

3. Paper Statements: If you see an envelope from your bank, don't worry, it's not a bill. Chances are, it's simply a statement that outlines your deposits, withdrawals, and account balances at the end of each month. A fee is becoming pretty common for this service. To get out of the fee, just go for the e-statements that you can access online for free. I find getting paper statements very annoying. I open them, read them, and end up throwing them out, since there's no immediate need for me to keep all that paperwork around. Go green and save some green while you're at it.

4. Check-Writing Fees: You'll usually get a free box of checks when you open your account, but after that, expect to pay up for some more checks. You'll pay $15–$25 for a new box of checks if you need to reorder. You might not write checks very often, but it's worth knowing that they aren't going to be free forever.

The days of free checking accounts are over. All you can do is anticipate the fees and try to find the least expensive options. According to the Merchants Payments Coalition, the average minimum balance needed to waive those minimum balance fees now stands at $391.21, as compared to $412.53 in 2011.[3] It's dropping, but if you think you'll have difficulty meeting that minimum, you need to find the bank that will penalize you the least.

The bottom line? Don't just walk into any bank and open up an account without understanding the bank's policies. Learn what you will be charged before you sign up. If there are fees, make sure you ask how you can avoid them. Transparency is a must (just like in the Presidential campaigns!).

If you're overwhelmed by the choices, try using the website FindABetterBank.com, which does exactly what its name says it does. Type in your zip code, answer some questions (do you want a bank with unlimited check writing or would you rather have a bank that has rewards attached to debit card usage?), and the site will find the bank that best suits your needs. Done and done!

Online Banks

You can do anything online these days—order food, buy books, and, yes, even do your banking in the comfort of your own home. If you're a technology fiend, an online bank might be the right choice for you. They have all the amenities of regular banks, but there are no physical branch locations where you can walk in and say hi to a teller.

Why would anyone put his or her money in an online bank? For one, the majority of online banks have *no* fees, not even minimum balance requirements.

And the interest rates are often higher. Think about it— the banks don't have to hire people to work in their branches, nor do they have to pay rent for those locations, so it's totally feasible for them to kick in an incentive to encourage consumers to bank online. We're not talking about dramatic increases though. Take HSBC, for example: its regular savings account offers 0.01 percent and its online savings account offers 0.40 percent, as of September 2012. Of course higher is better, but again these numbers are so low that the difference is almost negligible.

There are also some drawbacks to online-only banking. Any documents that need to be signed are typically sent back and forth by mail, including deposits, and most of the banks require *you* to pay for the postage.

Security when banking online is also a concern. Like any time you use the Internet, you want to make sure you take proper steps to ensure safety. First make sure you're banking with a reputable, FDIC-insured bank, not some random online bank where the security is questionable. And this is common sense, but please make strong passwords so it's tougher for thieves to hack in. No names or birthdays!

I don't bank online at the moment. I like being able to walk around the block and deposit a check in person. But maybe it's right for you.

Credit Unions

If you're fed up with the sneaky ways banks try to rip off consumers to make money, credit unions are a great alternative. A credit union is a not-for-profit financial institution formed and run by its members (that would be you if you joined one). Any profit made by the credit union is directed back to the members via lower interest rates on credit cards and higher interest rates on savings and checking accounts. Unlike regular banks, credit unions don't waste any money on lobbying or high executive bonuses, so they can offer more attractive benefits to their customers.

Credit unions have many of the same benefits as the big banks but without the hassles. Like banks, they have brick-and-mortar locations—that is, you can walk into one and talk to a teller. Some credit unions have online banking and some do not, so if that's important to you, do some research to see which credit unions in your area offer online services. The majority of credit unions are insured up to $250,000 by the National Credit Union Administration (similar to the FDIC), so your money is safe. Be mindful of the one-time member-ship fees at credit unions (typically between $5 and $10), but beyond that, when compared to traditional banks, their rates are better. The average credit union charges monthly fees of $6, whereas the average bank charges $10.27, according to a *Consumer Reports* study.[4]

Ondine Irving operates the website CreditCardConnec-tion.org, which allows you to type in your zip code and find a credit union in your area. Irving also says, in a *US News & World Report* article, that "some credit unions will reimburse a limited number of outside ATM transaction fees per month."[5] The article stresses the importance of ensuring that your credit union is part of the CO-OP Network, which in-cludes twenty-eight thousand ATMs that don't charge fees.[6]

Paying with Plastic

Upon opening a checking account, your bank will issue you a debit card. A debit card allows you to make purchases by tapping into your checking account, so you don't always have to be withdrawing cash. In the past few years, debit cards have become increasingly popular. According to the Federal Reserve, the number of debit-card-related transactions in 2011 was 47.6 billion.[7]

Debit cards are a great alternative to paying with cash. They look very similar to credit cards, but when you use one you're not getting into debt because you're using your own money to pay for the item. When you use a debit card to purchase a $20 T-shirt at Banana Republic, for example, that $20 leaves your checking account and goes directly to Banana Republic.

Anytime you're at a store and use a debit card to pay for something, you'll need to enter a PIN (personal identification number) right after you swipe your card at the register. Why? For security! You determine the PIN—usually a four-digit number—and can change it anytime by calling up your bank. Don't share it with anyone, and you shouldn't have it written on a piece of paper in your wallet, for obvious reasons.

As for the debit card itself, the line of numbers across the front is the card's number and likewise should not be shared with anyone. Your name will be printed on the card along with the expiration date. On the back of the card, there will be a space for your signature, so, yes, pick up a pen and physically sign it. It's for security purposes, and, in fact, some stores won't let you use your debit card if it's not signed!

At the moment, you don't pay a fee when you swipe your debit card (although that could change in the future—banks are always looking for ways to make money!). The merchant (whatever store you're shopping in: Best Buy, Macy's, or your local deli), however, does pay a fee to the bank every time you swipe that debit card. These fees, called "interchange fees," have sparked a huge debate in Washington, one that indirectly affects us, the consumer. The average interchange fee used to be forty-four cents, meaning every time you swiped your card the merchant had to send forty-four cents to the bank.[8]

The Dodd-Frank Act mandated that these interchange fees be capped at twenty-four cents starting on October 1, 2011. This cap only applies to the big banks (with assets over $10 billion), and not to credit unions. The result, as a CardHub.com study suggests, is that big banks lost $8.4 billion in 2011.[9]

The idea was that merchants would save money by paying lower fees, and perhaps that savings would trickle down to the consumer in the form of lower prices at the stores. A May 2012 article on Time.com examined this issue and concluded that consumers aren't seeing the savings, primarily because not all retailers are paying lower interchange fees yet.[10] The article cites an InternetRetailer.com survey that showed just 14.6 percent of retailers are paying lower fees—at that rate, who knows when consumers will see the benefit.

Overdraft Fees

Debit cards aren't entirely without their drawbacks, of course. Enter the much-hated world of overdraft fees. An overdraft fee is charged when there isn't enough money in your bank account to complete a withdrawal, purchase, or transaction. The bank needs to loan you the difference—so if there's $200 in your account, but you withdraw $300, the bank temporarily loans you $100. In exchange for loaning you the price of your purchase, it charges you a fee, and a pretty hefty one at that! Currently, the median overdraft fee nationally is $28, a 10 percent jump since 2008.[11]

It's *very* easy to end up with an overdraft. And while it's also easy to check how much is in our accounts (hint: online banking!), we don't always do that. I'll never forget the time I was charged *three* overdraft fees in one day. Yeah, you read that right—my bank slaughtered me. The reason I was slammed with three fees? A sandwich, a taxi, and a subway fare card. I made three stupid purchases in one day when I didn't realize a check I had deposited hadn't cleared yet. There wasn't enough money in my account to cover these purchases, so the $39 I spent that day ended up costing me $144. Yes, as in I got hit with $105 in overdraft fees. Since this was my first experience with an overdraft fee, I called up my bank and asked them to waive the fees—and they did.

Because it's so easy to lose track of our finances, overdraft fees are a *huge* cash cow for banks. In 2011 alone, banks made $31.6 billion from these fees, and that was less than the $33.1 billion the same fees earned in 2010, according to

Moebs Services.[12] Banks don't like to talk about how valuable an asset these fees are to them—in fact, they present them as a *service*. Check out what they believe to be protective measures:

1. Standard Overdraft Plan: With this type of plan, any purchase made is approved, but you'll be charged a fee if you don't have the funds in your account. If you use your debit card to purchase an $80 pair of jeans, for instance, but you only have $50 in your bank account, an overdraft fee of $35 will apply. Those $80 jeans will cost you a cool $115. And as in my experience with the sandwich, cab, and subway fare, this fee is applied every time an overdraft occurs. So if you use your debit card to buy something at Target, and then buy gas, and then get a smoothie at Jamba Juice, you'll be charged *three* overdraft fees if there isn't enough money in your account to support those purchases.

2. Overdraft Protection Services: In this case, the bank uses funds from your savings account to complete a transaction if you don't have enough in the account linked to your debit card. So if you have $25 in your checking account, but you're using your debit card to purchase a $30 case for your iPhone, the bank will take $5 from your savings account to complete the purchase. Or sometimes the bank will give you a loan (at a very high interest rate) for the difference between the value of the purchase (or withdrawal) and what's currently in your checking account—in this case a loan for $5. A $10 fee is typically applied too.

Banks acts as if these options are very helpful to consumers. Give me a break! They only cost the consumer money. A Pew Charitable Trusts study found that 60 percent of consumers who have overdrawn their account think their bank's overdraft policy "hurts more than helps."[13]

Thanks to new Federal Reserve laws, which took effect on August 15, 2010, when you overdraft on your account (either from using your debit card or from an ATM withdrawal), you will not be automatically enrolled in your bank's "standard overdraft plan" unless you give it permission to enroll you (aka unless you opt in). Instead your transaction will be *declined*, to prevent you from overdrawing your account and being charged the fee. Note that these laws don't apply to checks or automatic bill payments (that is, when you pay a company or service, like the electric company, automatically from your checking account), so the standard overdraft plan could still apply in those cases.

Now, you may be thinking, why would anyone let their banks enroll them in the standard overdraft plan? The Pew study found that 75 percent of respondents would rather have a purchase/withdrawal declined than be charged a $35 fee, but 18 percent didn't mind the fee.[14] Go figure. Some people would rather not face the embarrassment of having a cashier announce (loudly, so everyone else can hear!) that your debit card got declined. Count me in with the 75 percent. If my purchase or ATM withdrawal gets declined, I need to swallow my pride and realize that I'm not paying close enough attention to my finances.[15]

Bottom line? Educate yourself about your bank's overdraft fees. Don't opt in for overdraft protection, since there are fees attached. And, most important, always keep tabs on your checking account to keep from overdrawing or having your transaction declined.

If Your Debit Card Is Stolen

Thanks to the Federal Trade Commission, you are protected if your debit card is stolen or someone gets their hands on your number and PIN, but only up to a certain point.[16]

You should let your bank or card issuer know *as soon as possible* that your card or info was stolen. If you let your bank know within two business days that your card has gone missing, you'll only be responsible for a maximum of $50 worth of charges that someone else has made. But if you wait more than two business days to report the missing card, you could be responsible for a maximum of $500.

Now, let's say you didn't realize your card was stolen until you saw the suspicious charge on your bank statement. If you hadn't reported it stolen by that point, you could be liable for *all* the unauthorized charges. If you still have the actual debit card, but someone got hold of the number, then you're responsible for any charges that took place sixty days after the bank statement that shows the unauthorized activity was mailed to you or made available to you online.

Face it, in normal circumstances there's no reason for more than a couple of days to pass before you realize your card or info was stolen. If you can't find your debit card, report it missing. You should always examine your bank statements for fishy purchases, and since it only takes a minute, you'll feel much better if you do it every day.

Prepaid Debit Cards

Now let's talk about prepaid debit cards, which could quite possibly be the dumbest financial invention on the planet, and don't let anyone try to convince you otherwise.

If you were going to buy an $8 sandwich for lunch, would you want to pay an additional fee just to use your own cash? Uh, no! Well, that's how a prepaid debit card works. You fill up the card with money and spend it later, but you pay a bunch of fees along the way, including:

1. A monthly fee of approximately $10
2. A $2 fee to load money on the card
3. A dormancy fee (if you don't use the card for a certain period of time) of $5

Need I say more? They're a rip-off. And banks love them because the interchange fee cap that we just went over does not apply to prepaid debit cards—a nice loophole in the law that makes the banks more money.

Prepaid debit cards have been marketed as an alternative to checking accounts. A report from Javelin Strategy and Research suggests that use of these cards jumped by 18 percent in 2011.[17] One of the reasons for the increase in prepaid debit card usage could be—and this is just my humble opinion—

the fact that celebrities have been putting their faces on the cards to entice people to use them (think Russell Simmons, Alex Rodriguez, and, yes, the Kardashians, although Kim, Kourtney, and Khloe wisely canceled their prepaid card program once they realized how much of a rip-off it was). Ignore the celebs. When you look at the fees you'll pay for a prepaid debit card, it's clear that you'll only lose money. Go for the checking account (or credit union), and keep your money there rather than putting it on a prepaid debit card.

CDs

While we're on the subject of banks, I want to bring up a safe investment vehicle called a certificate of deposit (CD). Like savings accounts, CDs pay interest. As for the differences between a saving account and a CD, well, there are two: First, the interest rate on a CD is a bit higher than on money in a savings account. Second, your money is locked up for as long the CD lasts, whether three months, six months, one year, two years, or five years. The longer the duration of the CD, the higher the interest rate. CDs are a great tool if you are the type of person who feels tempted to dip into your savings account. Because you can't access your money until the CD expires, you can't spend it. It's a guaranteed way to save money.

Penalty Rates

Some CDs let you withdraw your money at any time without a penalty, but their interest rates tend to be lower. The typical penalty for early withdrawal is 60–180 days worth of interest, depending on the term of the CD. Sometimes the penalty amounts to more than the interest you've earned from the CD, and in such cases the bank may dip into the principal (the original amount you put into the CD) to pay for the penalty. Bottom line? If you use a CD, don't touch that money until the term has expired.

While CDs are a secure way to store (and save!) your money, you're not going to get rich off them, nor are they a reliable investment if you are trying to save for retirement. The interest rates are so low that after you factor in the taxes you'll pay on the money you made from the paltry interest rate and inflation (that's how much the price of goods rises every year, currently around 2–3 percent), you may actually earn a *negative interest rate*. Yup, that means you're losing money.

So when should you use a CD? In my opinion, you should use a CD if you're constantly tempted to pull money out of your savings account or you're too nervous to throw your money into riskier investments like stocks, bonds, and mutual funds. The last thing you want to happen is that you can't sleep at night because you purchased a volatile (risky) stock and you're worried that you're going to lose a lot of money.

While riskier investments offer greater rates of return, you don't want to put yourself into an ongoing state of a panic.

How to Make the Most of a CD

The way to make the most money in a CD is to do what's known as "laddering" it, or spreading it over different CDs with different term lengths. So if you have $2,000 you'd like to put away, instead of investing all of it in one CD, consider spreading it out into fourths:

$500 in a four-year CD at 2.5 percent
$500 in a three-year CD at 2 percent
$500 in a two-year CD at 1.5 percent
$500 in a one-year CD at 1 percent

When the term of the one-year CD expires, or "matures," you can elect to use the money to purchase a CD that has a longer term but a higher interest rate. Based on the example above, your total investments would have grown to $2,180.80. If you had dumped your original $2,000 into one one-year CD, your money would have only grown to $2,081.21. By laddering CDs, you earned an extra $100. Not bad! If you're interested in doing this but the math is making your head spin, no sweat—there are plenty of free CD laddering calculators online. A quick Google search will send you in the right direction.[18]

Quick Review

We just went over a ton of different options to keep in mind when picking a bank and using debit cards. Here's what you should remember:

1. Pick a bank with the lowest fees possible. Make sure you meet the bank's minimum balance requirement, so you don't get charged a fee.
2. Don't opt in for your bank's overdraft protection.
3. Know that you don't have to be a customer of a big bank. Credit unions tend to be friendlier and less costly.
4. Stay away from prepaid debit cards—they're not reliable and they'll only cost you money.
5. Be conscious of the low interest rates on savings accounts and CDs. They won't make you rich, but they could be a good tool if you're risk averse.

3

SAVING WITH STYLE: LIVE BIG ON NO MONEY

Oh, if only I could adequately describe the annoyed look that crossed a cashier's face when I whipped out my iPhone so she could scan a whole bunch of mobile coupons. And you know who was more pissed than the cashier? The old women in line behind me, who couldn't fathom that they had to wait for the cashier to scan a *smartphone*. I was just trying to save some money, ladies! No need to get all worked up.

We've been talking about the need to reduce certain areas of your budget, and, don't get me wrong, it's important. But just because you have to spend less to reach your financial goals, doesn't mean you have to sit inside every weekend and watch reruns of *The O.C.* You shouldn't have to compromise your lifestyle because you're low on cash. You just need to become a savvy shopper.

In this chapter, I'm going to cover how to use tools that are out there to help you save money in a big way. And there are way more of them than you think!

Extreme Couponing

Have you ever seen TLC's *Extreme Couponing*? It's incredible: the show documents people who obsessively cut and collect coupons, go on a shopping spree, and walk out of the store with several hundred bucks worth of loot while only paying $10 or $20 out of their pocket. These crazy couponers purchase so many items that they wind up having mini grocery stores in their basements, with hundreds of rolls of paper towels, dozens of jars of peanut butter (gross!), and enough bars of soap to last years. I sure as hell can't fit ten bottles of salad dressing in my studio apartment. Still, that's not to say there's nothing to learn from these techniques. Couponers bring up a central point when it comes to saving money: you should avoid paying full price whenever you can.

In *Extreme Couponing*, people obtain multiple copies of the Sunday newspaper. They either have them delivered or buy several copies at their local convenience store. Then they flip through the circulars, picking out the coupons they'll use—fifty cents off cereal here, $1 off shampoo there—and save them for a big shopping trip. Using the store circular, they figure out, for example, what's on sale in their local grocery store and then try to apply the coupons they have accumulated during weeks and weeks of clipping, making for a huge discount, a free product, or sometimes having the store pay *them* to buy something (like buying a pack of razors and the store gives them seven cents for it!). It's genius! They're buying an item that's on sale, and they're applying coupons to it too.

Now, I'm not saying that it's practical for all of us to hoard coupons for months and months. We can't all live on ramen because we're waiting to buy discounted cereal, after all. But here are some steps these coupon masters use that you can adopt to save a couple of bucks along the way:

1. Use a store coupon and a manufacturer's coupon at the same time, and you'll quickly become an expert at the art of coupon stacking. A store coupon is from the retailer itself (like the big purple coupons you might get in the mail from Bed Bath & Beyond that give 20 percent off any item in the store), while a manufacturer's coupon is from, well, the manufacturer and is for one of its specific products (like Dial soap, Gillette shaving cream, or Colgate toothpaste). So if you go to buy paper towels at Walgreens armed with a coupon for 10 percent off any item at Walgreens (that's a store coupon) *and* a coupon for $1 off a package of Bounty paper towels (that's a manufacturer's coupon), you'll receive both discounts. Not all stores allow stacking, but you can check out the store policy online (Walgreens, by the way, allows it).

2. The second technique is to shop at stores that will give you double your coupon's value. This means that if you have a coupon for $0.75 off a tube of Crest toothpaste, some stores will offer $1.50 off. Each store has a different policy when it comes to doubling coupons—some only offer it on certain days and hours of the week and some don't offer it at all. A quick check on their website will clear this up for you.

3. Finally, when you see something that you normally purchase (a staple item) on sale, stock up on it. I'm talking about soap, peanut butter, toilet paper, paper towels, or even your favorite brand of ice cream. Don't buy so much that you need to rent out another room to store it in, but buying a few extra bottles of your favorite conditioner when it's on sale is a wise idea. Hey, if you run out of room, you can always figure out some creative storage methods (a friend of mine stored T-shirts in his refrigerator when he ran out of room).

Coupon Apps

You don't need to spend time clipping physical coupons when you have digital ones at your fingertips.

Apps like Yowza!!, CouponSherpa, and RetailMeNot allow you to find mobile coupons right on your phone. The apps feature coupons for places like Amazon.com, Domino's Pizza, Target, Macy's, Forever 21, Six Flags, and JC Penney.

The best part is that you don't need to print them out to use them in a store. The cashier can scan the bar code that appears on the phone's screen and give you the discount. No clipping, printing, or lugging around a huge binder full of coupons necessary!

How Stores Trick Us into Buying More

Stores exist to make money, so you better believe they are going to try every sneaky tactic in the book to get consumers to spend more of it. Just like in a casino, the house always wins!

Whether it's where the escalators are positioned or the height of the shelves, stores are constructed strategically so consumers are always barraged with products and reminded to buy, buy, buy.

Let's say you need to make a quick run to the grocery store to pick up two items: a gallon of milk and a dozen eggs. Should be an easy task, right? Not when you're navigating the visual minefield that is a grocery store. You start walking to the back of the store, cutting down the cereal aisle, and, bam! Cocoa Krispies. You haven't had them since you were a kid! So, being the adult you are, you toss a box into the basket. You grab the milk and eggs next, but on your way back up the chips aisle you throw in a bag of Tostitos. And, hey, if you have tortilla chips, you might as well pick up an avocado—you can make guacamole when your friends come over later. Then just when you think you're done shopping, you start flipping through *People*, and, what the heck? You deserve a little light reading while on the elliptical, so you throw that in too.

See what I'm saying? Stores are *designed* to make us buy more. Staple items like bread, milk, and eggs are located in the back of the building, so shoppers have to walk through a maze of aisles to access that section. From the business point of view, the goal is to keep us in the store for as long as possible, to increase the probability that we'll buy more. The more we see, the more we're tempted to add to our carts. And we all do it! We pass an item that looks good—the Cocoa Krispies, the Tostitos—and add it to our shopping cart, even if we didn't come into the store to buy it.

Ready for another grocery store trick? Items on the shelf that are eye level are typically the more expensive items. Think about it: you're not going to be buying something on the top shelf that you can't reach—and you're probably not going to bend down to grab an item on the very bottom shelf. But you should—because the items on the top and bottom shelves are typically cheaper.

Be a Savvy Shopper

There are some other little tricks that grocery stores have to make you spend more. I bet you've seen them advertise a sale like "ten yogurts for $10." Most people start loading up their baskets with more than their arms can handle, but here's the catch: you don't need to buy ten to get the discount. The store will honor that $1 per yogurt price even if you only buy two or three. Some stores may have a minimum, but if you check the fine print, it usually isn't the full quantity. Stores do this as a way to clear out inventory and encourage consumers to buy more.

The best way to save at the store is undeniably simple: write down what you need before you leave the house. Making a list is bound to save you money by preventing impulse shopping. A study from the University of Pennsylvania's Wharton School showed that if you don't plan out your trip to the grocery store, your unplanned purchases increase some 23 percent.[1] So take five minutes and write down the items you need, and then, most important, once you get to the store don't stray from the list—otherwise, what's the point of having one?

The Lure of Sales

Another way stores try to persuade us to buy more is by throwing around words like "sale" and "clearance." Sales tend to be for a certain period of time (maybe for just one day or for the Fourth of July weekend), whereas items on a clearance rack remain discounted until sold. Either way, stores do this for the same reason: to subconsciously influence you to buy.

The word "sale" automatically instills a sense of urgency in the potential buyer. Let's say you purchased a jacket a few months ago. When you walk into a store to buy a new pair of jeans, you probably aren't even thinking about jackets. But when you see another nice jacket that's "on sale," you might be more apt to consider purchasing it than you would have been if there was no sign. Buying that jacket and pretending to be a smart shopper is one of the worst financial moves you can make. You just bought a jacket—why are you buying another one? Because it's on sale? Come on! "On sale" doesn't mean it's free.

When does it make sense to buy something on sale? When you truly need it and the sale price is reasonable enough that it doesn't throw off your budget. In that case, you have identified a need and fulfilled it in a cost-conscious way. Don't fall prey to the signs.

What If an Item Goes on Sale Right After You Buy It?

It happens to the best of us: you buy something, only to discover a few days later that the same item is on sale and you missed out. Annoying, right?

If this happens, take the item back to the store and ask for a price adjustment, showing the cashier your receipt as proof. If you buy a pair of pants for $70 and three days later notice those same pants are on sale for $50, bring them back to the store with the receipt, and it should refund you the difference (in this case, $20). Each store will have a different policy—usually you can only receive adjustments fifteen to thirty days after you made the purchase.

This happened to me recently. I bought a new printer, and when it went on sale the *next day*, I was kicking myself, so I called up the retailer's customer service line (since I had ordered the printer online), and told them what happened. After only a few minutes of discussion, the representative ended up crediting me the difference between what I paid and the sale price. If you get in this situation, just explain it like this:

"I'm calling because I ordered a Hewlett-Packard printer yesterday on Staples.com and today I noticed the same printer is on sale for $15 less than what I paid. I was wondering if I could get a price adjustment." As long as you're honest and direct, you have an excellent shot at getting that $15 back in your pocket.

Have you heard of the website Hukkster.com? The site lets you download a button for your web browser, known as the "Hukk It" button. The button lets you know when the price of a certain item drops. So let's say you're eyeing a new pair of shoes on Macys.com, but you don't want to pay the full price. Simply add the item to your list on Hukkster.com, set the current price, and when the item goes on sale or is discounted, you'll be the first to know via an alert. Easy, right?

And while you're on the hunt for bargains, download the Decide smartphone app. This app uses an algorithm to track price movements of electronics and appliances. So if you're in the market for a fancy new TV set, you can pull up that item on the app, and it will tell you if you should buy the item now or wait, based on a prediction of whether the item will go on sale in the near future.

Comparison Shopping

Ever hear how major electronics stores like Best Buy are the showrooms for Amazon.com? In this age of technology, people head to Best Buy to see an item in person but end up buying it on Amazon to get a better deal. This approach is effective, but if you're like me—someone who doesn't want to pay for shipping or wait several days for the item to arrive— you prefer shopping at the brick-and-mortar stores. Don't worry—you can still pay the online prices even if you are in a physical store.

How do you do it? Comparison shopping. It's not an Earth-shattering concept, but with a technological twist, it's probably the best (and easiest) approach to use to get your desired price. Using your smartphone, specifically the free ShopSavvy app (available for the iPhone and Android phones), scan the bar code of any item in any store, and the app will find the retailer (even the online ones) that sells the item for the lowest price. Say you're in Best Buy, looking to buy a digital camera, and the app tells you that both Amazon and a store a few miles away sell the exact same camera for less. Before you run down the road to the other store, try doing this:

1. Walk up to a salesperson, or even the store manager, and show them your smartphone. Explain that you found out that the other store is selling the same product for X dollars, but you'd like to do business at this store (Best Buy, in this case).

2. Ask him to match the price. You're presenting proof (the info from the app), and if the salesperson or their manager agrees, you'll be able to buy the item right then and there while paying the competitor's lower price. Beautiful, right?

Plenty of consumers are following this technique. A survey from the Interactive Advertising Bureau suggests that 30 percent of shoppers with mobile phones decided against a purchase while in a store because they found a better price online, and 38 percent did the same because they found a better price at another store.[2]

Discounted Gift Cards

Gift cards: they're awesome to use when they're for a store you like and impossible to get rid of when they're for one you hate. But now, thanks to some innovative websites, those unused cards no longer have to linger in your wallet.

Say your dear aunt Ida gives you a $100 Home Depot gift card for your birthday, but you wouldn't know the difference between a wrench and a hammer if it hit you in the face. No need to walk around aimlessly in the lighting section pretending to be interested in light fixtures. Instead you can sell your gift card for up to 90 percent of its value at websites like PlasticJungle.com and CardPool.com.

These sites will give you up to $80 for your $100 Home Depot gift card, and then they'll sell it to someone else who's willing to pay $90. Everyone wins! (Except maybe Aunt Ida.) You get cash for a gift card you were never going to use, the website makes a $10 profit, and someone else who spends their Friday nights in the plumbing section of Home Depot is going to be able to get $100 worth of plastic pipe at a 10 percent savings.

On the flip side, searching these sites for discounted gift cards for your favorite stores is a great way to save 5–25 percent. I'm talking major stores and major discounts. The last time I perused the site, I saw deals for 5 percent off an iTunes card, 15 percent off a Kohl's gift card, 6 percent off a Best Buy card, and 18 percent off at California Pizza Kitchen. So next time you're thinking about making a purchase at a department store or are heading to dinner at a restaurant, check out the discounted gift card websites first. The cards can either be sent via mail (a bit time-consuming, so choose this option if you know what you want to buy in advance) or the website can e-mail you the card's code (better for those last-minute dinner plans).

Come on—this is such an easy way to save!

While we're on the subject of gift cards, just know that a provision in the Federal Credit CARD Act of 2009 states that gift cards cannot expire until five years have passed since the card was opened. We'll go into this a bit more in the next chapter, but in the meantime you have only five years to use those gift cards. What are you waiting for?

Promotional Codes

Most of the time, when you make a purchase online, I guarantee you're missing out on savings. How? Those ever-elusive promotional codes!

When you're shopping online and are about to check out, you'll often see a box asking you to enter a "coupon code" or "promotional code." If you're like most people, you probably skip over that box, figuring that no matter how many times you smash the buttons on your keyboard or type in a random combination of letters and numbers, you won't crack the code.

Well, guess what? If you're able to master the simple task of Googling, it's actually pretty easy to find that magic combination of numbers and letters.

I wasn't always a promo-code-cracking sleuth. Every time I ordered my contact lenses online, I would pay the full price and wonder who the heck ever got the promotional code. I certainly never did. So the last time I ordered them, I was determined not to click on Submit Order until I found one. And I did! And it was easier than I thought. I Googled "1-800 Contacts coupon code" and instantly found a code. Okay, so the first code I tried didn't work, but I went back to the Google page and found another code. I entered it in the box and bam! The price went from $100 to $95—not bad for twenty seconds of work!

To make this process even easier, websites like Retail MeNot.com and PromotionalCodes.com focus solely on finding coupon codes. Other sites pull up codes so you can avoid paying shipping costs. FreeShipping.org boasts free shipping codes to more than four thousand stores, like Target, Amazon, Kohl's, and Nordstrom. You'll never have to skip those promo codes again!

Your E-mail Makes You Spend, Not Save

We can't talk about coupons and saving money without discussing sites like Groupon and LivingSocial (and we can't forget Yipit, which lists aggregated deals from all the social-couponing sites).

These sites aren't inherently bad (hey, I got a $10 haircut

from a deal on Groupon), but they tend to cause us to spend money on stuff we wouldn't normally buy. E-mail from Groupon and LivingSocial is a major impetus to impulse spending. In fact, an ExactTarget survey showed that 66 percent of American web users have made a purchase because of an e-mail.[3]

A lot of us are addicted to checking e-mail, and if we see an e-mail from Groupon that features a bunch of items or vacations on sale, we're likely to consider buying what's advertised. I used to subscribe to the Groupon e-mails, and every few days one would arrive that said, "Trip to Ireland—50 percent off. Includes hotel, meals for two people." Every time I saw it, I thought about taking advantage of the deal, which is amazing, because without seeing this e-mail, booking a trip to Ireland would have never even come close to crossing my mind.

So with that I say, unsubscribe from e-mail, not only from Groupon, LivingSocial, and Yipit, but any other retailer's mailing list. It tends to nudge us in the direction of spending or buying things we don't need. This doesn't mean you shouldn't look at these services' websites, since they can be a huge help in certain situations. If you're going out to dinner with friends, for example, you can zero in on your area and see what restaurants are offering deals. Many times these deals will include discounted appetizers or drinks or even dinner for two, or four, which is great.

The bottom line? Maximize your savings by checking these sites, but don't subscribe to their daily e-mails.

Stop with the Wave and Pay

I'm not a huge Starbucks fan, but a little while ago it ran a two-week special where all Frappuccinos were half price. I know I told you earlier in this chapter to avoid succumbing to the pressure of sales, but, hey, things happen. I bring up this story because I was amazed at how the guy in front of me paid for his coffee. It wasn't with cash, it wasn't with a card—it was by using his phone. He just tapped his smartphone against a sensor and, just like that, he was done. I'd heard about this before, but seeing it in a store made me do a double take.

The Frap-happy guy in front of me was most likely doing this through Google Wallet, which allows users to pay just by tapping their phones. And it's not just smartphones that are replacing the act of swiping. The major credit card companies are now adding this technology to their credit and debit cards. MasterCard's PayPass is a prime example. At restaurants, stadiums, pharmacies, and grocery stores, you can simply tap your PayPass card against a sensor to pay for your items, no swiping or signing needed.

This may be convenient and efficient, but studies show that contactless payment technology results in higher spending—a 30 percent jump in spending, according to a MasterCard Advisors study.[4] What is more fascinating is that the 30 percent increase was the same for all incomes. Whether the person was a big spender or a penny pincher before using the technology, contactless pay resulted in the same increase. In some cases, the study found that people spent an extra $600 a month as a result of contactless pay.

You see where I'm going with this: don't use contactless pay! Yes, it's cooler than swiping a credit card or handing over a dirty piece of paper with Andrew Jackson's face on it, but you're going to spend more, regardless of your spending habits or your budgeting skills. An extra thirty seconds at the register won't kill you.

Dining Out

As mentioned in the first chapter, going out to restaurants can eat away a huge chunk of your income. I understand why it's so tempting. It's much easier to order takeout than to cook and wash dishes. And it's a lot more fun to head to a new restaurant on a Friday night, with friends, than to sit alone at home with a bowl of soup.

I'm not saying don't eat out. After all, I don't want to kill your social life. But I want to mention one more study, which might make you reconsider how often you eat out. A March 2012 Harris Interactive study showed that 36 percent of Americans eat out on most nights but go to lower priced restaurants, while 29 percent are willing to reduce other areas of their budget to be able to eat out (oh, those die-hard foodies!).[5] If you're spending a huge portion of your budget on eating out, it's best to look at ways to help curb your spending without curbing your appetite.

The best way to save money on restaurants is by purchasing those discounted gift cards I mentioned above (they are mostly for national chain restaurants) or to check out your Groupon and LivingSocial accounts for restaurant deals in your neck of the woods.

But I've got another option for you to try: cook food at home three nights a week for one month and see how you like it. This challenge will help give you perspective on just how much you spend on takeout and restaurants. You may end up realizing you have a talent for it!

If cooking at home doesn't do it for you, be creative in cutting your costs. How about hosting a dinner party instead of hitting up the newest restaurant in town? Have each of your friends bring a dish, and everyone can share the food. (I'll bring the pasta!) This will be much cheaper than going out to a restaurant, and it's a nice change of pace from the normal routine of going out. If you're not much of a host, try meeting your friends for a late breakfast on the weekend instead of a fancy dinner on Friday night. Breakfast is a lot cheaper than dinner.

Even if salads and steaks suit you more than scrambled eggs and yogurt, just try out some these ideas for a month. See how it goes. You might find that you'd rather cut down spending in other areas so you can afford to go out to eat, or you might discover that you're the next Iron Chef and dedicate yourself to cooking at home more often. You know, making sense of your personal finances is really about experimentation and moderation. I'd be curious to see how your budget changes when you try implementing these cheaper dining ideas (and I'm sure it'll result in saving money!).

Who Pays?

Ever go out to a restaurant with friends and you order just one dish, while some of your friends order a soda, appetizer, main dish, and dessert? When the check comes, it's always an uncomfortable race to figure out the bill. A lot of times, people will suggest splitting the bill equally, even if that's not fair.

The easiest way to avoid paying for your friend's dessert is to ask your waiter or waitress for a separate check at the beginning of the meal. If the restaurant doesn't offer separate checks, tell your friends to split up the bill by dish. Even if it is awkward to say, it's fair to do.

Restaurants aren't the only places where payment problems can arise. Groceries can present issues too. If you live with roommates and they keep eating the food you bought, you're bound to get pissed. Best advice? Make it a house rule that everyone buys and eats their own groceries. It sounds selfish, but arguing with your roommates over money is never fun.

Slash Your Cell Phone Bill

Cell phones are another major expense, often costing over $50 a month. And with smartphones, we're now also paying for Internet access and e-mail, which makes it even more costly.

Take a look at these tricks to cut the cost of your bill. There's a good chance you're overpaying. Ask yourself the following questions about your cell phone:

1. Do I Have the Right Plan? You don't want to be paying for minutes you don't use. Call up your cell phone company and ask it to access your account history to see how many minutes you've been using. If you constantly have hundreds left over, then it's time to switch to a plan with fewer minutes.

A great way to find the picture-perfect plan is to use BillShrink.com. It'll mean answering several basic questions, like:
- Who is your current provider?
- Are you under contract? For how long?
- How many months remain on your contract?
- What do you pay right now for your monthly cell phone service?
- Do you text? Do you need e-mail/Internet access for your phone?
- What is your zip code?

In just a few minutes, the site will find the cheapest carriers in your area that suit your needs.

2. Am I a Loyal Customer? Have you been with your carrier for many years? Do you constantly pay on time? If so, that means you're a loyal customer and you deserve a reward, right? Call up Verizon, AT&T, or whatever wireless service you use, and ask for a loyalty credit. Yes, you can do this, and, yes, there's a strong chance you will get it. It could be $100 or $150, but it's literally free money, just for being a good customer. So take two minutes and make this phone call.

Remember, the company doesn't want to lose your business, so giving you an incentive to stay is in its best interest too.

3. Do I Want to Extend My Contract? If you plan on living in your current area for several more years, it might make sense to call up your provider and offer to extend your contract in exchange for a discount. Simply say to the customer service representative that you're happy with the service and want to lengthen your contract for another year, and—here's the kicker—you'd like a discount for offering to extend your contract. More often than not, the rep will offer you one, and you can always ask for a supervisor if the rep isn't being forthcoming about it.

4. Will I Be Using the Phone Abroad? Whether you are going on a safari in Africa or are backpacking through Europe, if you plan on using your cell phone abroad, it's best to check with your carrier about the costs, before you go. Roaming charges can add up exponentially if you're not careful. Most major cell phone providers have plans that allow international use for a few extra dollars a month.

Keep in mind that canceling your cell phone contract often comes with a nice cancelation fee, as high as $175. So before you fire your cell phone provider, make sure you're doing it without having to pay for the trouble.

Using Your Student ID

College and graduate students have a secret weapon: the student ID card. It's one of the best coupons you could ever dream of, offering discounts at stores, movie theaters, museums, and restaurants. All you have to do is flash your ID, and voilà! The discount is yours.

Here Are Some of the Best Deals:

- Shopping addict? J. Crew and Banana Republic offer students 15 percent off, and Ann Taylor and Club Monaco offer 20 percent off.

- Do you take Amtrak? If so, Amtrak offers a student discount—15 percent off most train rides.[6]

- Any interest in reading the *Wall Street Journal*? Students can subscribe to the paper for 75 percent less than the regular rate. (And your friends will be impressed if a *Wall Street Journal* is delivered to your dorm room!)

- Are you majoring in graphic design and need to purchase those expensive programs from Adobe? Adobe offers hefty discounts to students. The Creative Suite 5.5 Master Collection sells for $2,599, but you'll pay only $899.

- Don't forget about the student discounts Apple and Microsoft typically offer. During summer 2011, any student who purchased a Windows 7 PC got a free Xbox 360, and Apple was giving a $100 gift card for its App Store.

Local stores and restaurants may offer student discounts too—don't be afraid to ask!

Saving Money on Textbooks

Heads up: if you've been buying textbooks at your school's bookstore, you are getting ripped off—big time.

Here Are Some Strategies to Cut That Textbook Bill in Half:

1. Find the Cheapest Textbook Retailers: On my website, HelpSaveMyDollars.com, I have a free textbook search engine (HelpSaveMyDollars.com/Textbooks), which compares prices from over fifty different retailers, including those that do textbook rentals. I rented an accounting textbook for $53 that would have cost over $200 to purchase—not bad for a few minutes of work.

2. Buy Used Textbooks: I saved nearly $200 by purchasing used textbooks. Check out eBay's Half.com to search for used books.

3. Rent Textbooks: Once the class is over, you don't need the textbook anymore. Visit Chegg.com to rent textbooks. Instead of buying a $100 book, you could rent it for $30–$40.

4. Sell Your Textbooks: At the end of the semester, sell your textbooks online to recover some of the cost of buying them.

> You can even sell your textbooks back to Amazon .com, which will buy them for up to 70 percent of their value and give you an Amazon.com gift card for the amount. Hey, Amazon gift cards are as good as cash these days!

5. Trade Books with Other Students: You may not need your history textbook from last semester, but plenty of other students probably do. Use TextSwap.com to trade books with other students.

6. International Editions: You can sometimes save over 70 percent by purchasing the international version of a textbook. Visit TextbooksRus.com to search for international editions.

Also, try to find out exactly why you'll need the textbook. In my calculus class during freshman year, I only needed the book for homework problems, so I shared it with a friend and we split the price. You may have to wait a few classes to see what role the textbook will play.

And if you're in a bind and simply cannot afford a textbook, explain your situation to your professor to see if there is an extra copy available that could be loaned to you (or you can check your school's library!).

Textbooks on the Kindle and iPad

What if you don't want to carry forty pounds of textbooks around campus? If you have a Kindle or an iPad, you're in luck. You can save yourself the back pain and hundreds of dollars simply by renting books on e-readers.

Amazon.com is now offering e-textbooks for the Kindle. With Kindle Textbook Rental, you can save 80 percent. If you have an iPad, the Inkling app allows you to purchase specific chapters from textbooks. The app also features quizzes and assessments, to help you study.

How Congress Is Helping Students
Save Money on Textbooks

You read that right: Congress has passed legislation that helps students save money on books. Thanks, Congress!

The law aims to provide more transparency and fairness in the textbook industry. It took effect on July 1, 2010, as part of the Higher Education Opportunity Act of 2008.[7] Here are the two main highlights:

1. Universities must provide a price list of required textbooks and their ISBN numbers at the time students enroll for classes. This will give students time to shop around and compare prices at different retailers.

2. Some publishers had bundled textbooks with CDs and additional workbooks. This law requires publishers to sell each item separately, allowing students to buy only what they need.

Unfortunately, not all bookstores are up to date with these laws. Last semester I had to buy a huge set of textbooks for a finance class. I would have paid $192 at my school's bookstore for the main textbook, a workbook, and an answer key, all bundled together in plastic. I didn't want to buy them together because I knew I could get the main textbook for under $100 if I rented it online. So I asked the bookstore staff if they knew about the law forbidding bundles, and they looked at me like I was crazy! After speaking to the manager, however, they allowed me to buy only the workbook and answer key, instead of the entire package. I then ordered the main textbook and saved about $50. So if your school's bookstore hasn't caught on to this law, kindly inform them! You'll end up saving yourself some much-needed green.

Quick Review

Now that you're equipped with some savvy savings strategies, here are the key takeaways:

1. Get couponing! Whether it's online promotional codes, coupon apps, or thumbing through the newspapers, don't underestimate the value of this free money.
2. Buying discounted gift cards before you shop is a guaranteed way to save 5–25 percent on purchases.
3. Stop subscribing to e-mails from stores and discount

sites. They will make you spend money on things you don't need. Check out the retailers' websites to get the deals without the constant reminders to buy.

4. Be conscious of some of your big-ticket expenses—restaurants, cell phone, utilities—and use the strategies discussed to reduce them.

5. If you're a student, use your ID to your advantage! There are tons of discounts available to you.

4

NEVER PAY FULL PRICE FOR ANYTHING: NEGOTIATING 101

Okay, I admit it. In case you haven't guessed it already, I was a bit of a nerd in middle school: glasses, braces—the whole shebang. The story that probably best sums up my personality, then *and* now, involves buying a pair of glasses when I was around twelve. My mom was about to pay for them, and I interrupted the transaction—this twelve-year-old with a high-pitched voice—to ask the saleswoman if she could do any better on the price. My mom looked at me with such shock that you would think I had dropped an f-bomb.

Well, much to my mom's surprise, the woman took off $30, just like that! I realized that it pays to be the kid who pushes boundaries sometimes. I began incorporating this philosophy into other areas of my life, especially as I got older, whether it was bargaining with corner fruit vendors in New York City or asking for a room upgrade at hotels on vacations, and it has saved me a ton of money along the way. There's no reason you can't do it too!

In this chapter, we'll talk about the rules of bargaining.

Whether you're looking to buy clothes, a TV, or a car, the following techniques could save you a *ton* of money.

Always Ask, but Do It the Right Way

Negotiating and bargaining have been going on for as long as civilization has existed, but a lot of us are scared to do it. What's the worst that can happen? Someone says, "No, we can't do any better," to you? Seriously. It's not that traumatic or embarrassing of an experience.

Attitude is key when negotiating. Approaching a seller with a rude or arrogant disposition won't help your case. Think about it. If you're a store clerk and someone asks you for a discount in an argumentative tone, why would you go out of your way to do what they're asking? The objective is to be courteous to your "opponent" in any negotiating situation. A heated debate will only make the blood boil on both sides, and no one wants a headache. So keep it nice, will ya?

Go into it armed with information—you already know how to find competitive prices on your smartphone from chapter 3—and approach the situation confidently. It's key to speak to a decision maker—most likely a manager—rather than a regular employee, who may not have the power to offer a discount. It's as simple as asking the store clerk, "Can I speak to the manager?" Don't be afraid!

You're not *entitled* to the discount, but if you politely point out a competitor's price and say how you'd rather do business here, you're much more likely to be well received.

If an Item Is Damaged

I once bought a $100 dress shirt that was marked down to $50 on the clearance rack at a major department store. I examined it, to try to figure out why it was on clearance, and saw a small stain on the back of the shirt. You could barely see it, but if I'm going to pay $50 for a shirt, why should there be a stain on it? I showed the damage to the cashier and asked if a discount could be offered to me—and it was! The cashier gave me an additional 10 percent off because of the damage.

No matter what you're buying, whether you see a scuff on a pair of shoes or damage to the box the product is in (which is a sign that there could be damage to the actual product), speak up and ask for a discount!

Scoring Freebies

What's the next best thing after getting a discount? A freebie!

Whenever I get a new cell phone, I always ask for a free case or an extra charger. Cases could cost $30 and the charger could cost another $50. I've found that many cell phone companies are receptive to customers who ask for these little extras, so don't hesitate to try!

Live Big, Pay a Little Less

Negotiating a better rent is largely dependent on the real estate market in your area. If you happen to be looking for an apartment in what's known as a "seller's market" (when demand for housing is higher than the number of available houses or apartments), then you're at a disadvantage. The landlords and sellers know that if you won't buy or rent their place, someone else will, since the market is hot.

On the flip side, if you're in a "buyer's market," you are at a total advantage, since sellers are usually desperate, and there's plenty of inventory so they have a lot of competition. You can't control the housing market, so you have to make do with what you have.

During a buyer's market, you have a lot of negotiating power, and you can potentially get an incredible deal. However, we usually see buyer's markets during a recession, as was the case back in 2009. But as I write this, in 2012, some areas of the country are seeing seller's markets, especially in New York City, where there's a 1 percent vacancy rate and the average apartment rent is a staggering $2,900![1] Wow!

Regardless of what type of market you end up in, when it comes time to rent a house or apartment, you can start off by—wait for it—asking if the owner can do any better on the rent. This tactic will work a lot more effectively if you're trying to rent a house or apartment from an owner and not a major leasing company. A regular owner who's just trying to rent or sublet their apartment may be more flexible than a major landlord or leasing developer. You can always ask a landlord, but be prepared for less flexibility than you'll find with most individuals.

When you rent an apartment or house, you can typically lock into a one- or two-year lease. If you're in a buyer's market, you might want to consider signing the two-year lease. The real estate market can be hard to predict, so it's possible that one year it's a buyer's market, the next year it's a seller's market, and your rent could jump up. In case you're worried about the long term, try this creative alternative: When my father rented an apartment in New York City during the recession, he found a great deal on a place that would have cost $1,000 more a month had he rented it in a booming economy. So he signed a two-year lease to lock in that low price. But with the market still so unpredictable, he didn't want to be married to such a serious monthly expense for that length of time, so he asked the landlord to add a clause in the leasing contract/agreement that gave him the option to break the lease after one year, without any penalties or fees. And the landlord did it!

Now I doubt the landlord would have granted this clause had it been a strong economy, because he or she probably could have found another person willing to sign the lease without the one-year exit option. But, hey, it doesn't hurt to ask for this when signing a long-term lease.

Negotiating Extra Perks

Usually, the apartment or house you're about to rent will be painted by the landlord, but expect it to be plain, boring white. If you plan to paint the place anyway (and your lease allows it), ask the landlord to paint the place the color you want. In fact, you can even offer to buy the paint. Who the hell wants to waste a weekend painting their apartment?

As you get older and make more money, you may find yourself renting an apartment in a building that has a gym or other amenities. These buildings will usually charge you a fee on top of your monthly rent to use these facilities. Before you sign the lease, ask for a free gym membership for six months—what do you have to lose?

Hotel Rooms

Hotels are great places to score deals. Think about how much money you spend there—from the room itself to eating at the hotel's restaurants to paying to park your rental car in the hotel's garage. And think about what could go wrong when staying at a hotel, from a dirty room (or an iron that leaks grease all over your clothes—yep, that happened once!) to lost luggage or some jerk blasting techno music in the room next door. Do I even have to say this? Take the opportunity to negotiate a better price!

When you're booking the hotel room, you might use a travel site like Expedia, Orbitz, or Hotels.com, and that's fine. You may score a sweet deal. But you may also want to try booking the room through the hotel's reservation line. Ask the hotel rep if there are any sales or discounts that could be applied to your reservation. If one of those discount travel sites has a better deal than the hotel itself, which is sometimes the case, ask the hotel to *beat* the site's deal.

Arguably the most effective hotel-bargaining tactic is to ask for a room upgrade a few days before you arrive or when you're checking in. I remember my parents asking for a room upgrade whenever we checked into a hotel on vacations when I was a kid. Usually, the person at the front desk has some leeway to assign you a room on a higher floor or with a view of the ocean, for example, rather than one that faces the parking lot.

You may not be able to speak with the hotel's general manager when you check in, but what you can do is call the general manager a day or two before you arrive. Say you're thrilled to be staying at the hotel and want to know if it's possible to get an upgrade to a better room, perhaps even to a suite, for no additional charge.

Whether or not you get an upgrade, you know as well as I do that you're likely to run into some sort of issue during your stay—from a broken shower to a room that smells like cigarettes to crazy neighbors. Hotels take this stuff very seriously because now more than ever consumers have the power, via the Internet, to share their bad experiences with the world. Whether it's writing a poor review on TripAdvisor.com or creating a YouTube video, people are very willing to share their experiences with more than just family and friends, and hotels know that. You may never want to return to the hotel, and that's fine, but the last thing a hotel wants is negative press.

If there is a problem with the room, head back down to the front desk and ask to speak with the general manager. The hotel will obviously come and clean the room or try to fix the problem, but what it should do is offer you a freebie, such as free breakfast at the hotel restaurant for the rest of your vacation or, in some cases, a free night's stay. The latter is what you want to aim for. Remember, even if the situation is terrible, be polite to the general manager.

Airline Fees

Last summer I booked a trip to visit a friend in Florida about four weeks in advance. I got a pretty good deal on the airfare and was looking forward to going. But a week after I booked my flight, I realized that I had made a mistake: I had booked the flight a day early, which was the same day I was supposed to attend a relative's wedding. I called up the airline and explained the situation, telling the customer service rep that I wanted to move my flight to the next day.

I was concerned that I was going to get slammed with change fees, because you can't just switch your flight so easily: there are usually fees involved. Sure enough, it was $100 to change my flight! I politely asked the rep to waive the fee, since I've been a loyal customer, as have many friends and family members. The rep wasn't exactly eager to do it, so I politely asked to speak to a manager, who immediately waived the $100 change fee. Just like that! It was worth waiting on hold for about seven minutes to be transferred to a manager.

Job Offer

I want to end this negotiating chapter by talking about job offers. Here's where I chicken out when it comes to negotiating. If you get a job offer, especially if this is your first major job, take it and run! Don't be foolish and try to squeeze extra money out of the employer by asking for a higher salary before you even start the job. In these tough economic times, pushing the envelope, especially when it comes to your first job, is a bit risky. You don't want to come across as arrogant or entitled, which you know is already the stereotype of our generation.

Unless your starting salary is so low that you would need to take on a second job just to pay the rent, I would refrain from asking your prospective employer to "do better" on the salary offered to you. The time to ask for a raise is after a few years, when you've proven yourself as an indispensable asset to the company or organization where you work. If you've added noticeable value to the company—maybe you exceeded your sales goal if you're in a sales job or you conceived a brilliant idea for the organization's social media campaign—you have even more leverage in asking for a raise.

Quick Review

This was a fun chapter focused on asking just one question that can save you money: can you do better on the price? Remember these four key points when you negotiate:

1. Come on now, don't be afraid to ask for a deal. It's your hard-earned money at stake!
2. Research prices at competing stores. Showing proof that a competitor is offering an item for less will help you clinch the deal.
3. Think about who has more negotiating power, you or your opponent? If the advantage is in your hands, negotiate like a tiger!
4. Be polite! Nobody wants to help someone who is being angry or irrational.

5

EVERYTHING YOU NEED
TO KNOW ABOUT CREDIT

You know you've had this happen to you: you're sitting there, minding your business, when all of a sudden someone starts humming a jingle from a popular TV commercial. It's terrible. It's annoying. And now it *won't get out of your head.*

One of the worst offenders are the FreeCreditReport .com commercials, which have become so ingrained in us, such a part of our culture, that they have over *one million* views on YouTube. Who would think a YouTube clip with that many views would be about a credit score?!

The people in the FreeCreditReport.com commercials aren't the only ones who are uninformed when it comes to credit. In fact, I'll wager a bet that most people who watch that video on YouTube don't have a full understanding of what credit is. If you're one of those people, don't sweat it! Because this chapter is all about credit—what it is, why it's important, and how to manage yours.

What Is Credit?

When I was in high school, I thought it would be smart to get a credit card. The idea didn't come out of thin air. All my friends had them, thanks to their parents. Every time we went out, they would swipe, swipe, swipe their Visa card or MasterCard, while I was laying out bills on the table. My parents said no way to making me an authorized user on their card, so I decided to investigate how I could get that coveted piece of plastic myself, and that's when I discovered the term "building credit."

Credit is using other people's money. Anytime you hear about someone buying something on credit, it means that they're borrowing money with the intention to pay it back later. That's where credit cards come in. We'll get into more specifics about credit cards in the next chapter, but when you swipe your credit card to buy a new pair of shorts, you're not using your own money. You're using the credit card company's money, and you'll have to pay it back. For people our age, the main reason to use a credit card is to establish a credit history. Your credit history is the record of how well you use other people's money.

If you ever want to get a loan to buy a car or to get a mortgage later on in life, your credit history lets lenders gauge whether you are a risky customer. Think about it: The bank that loans you money is taking a risk. It doesn't know if you're going to pay back the loan. But your credit history lets the bank in on critical information about you and your past financial habits that can help it decide whether or not to lend to you.

Your credit history includes what's known as a "credit report" and a "credit score." Let's talk about the credit report first. Think of your credit report as a financial transcript. Here's what I mean: when you were applying for college, you had to send the prospective university a high school transcript, which lists all the classes you took and the grades you received in them. The college used the info on your transcript to help decide whether you were qualified to be accepted into the college. Well, when you're applying for credit—whether it's a credit card, a car loan, or a mortgage—a similar process of vetting occurs. Just like a high school transcript reveals your academic qualifications, a credit report reveals your financial qualifications. A credit report is a summary of your recent financial and credit transactions. It'll show all your past and current credit cards, loans, mortgages, or lines of credit that have been associated with you, starting with your first credit card.

A creditor (the company giving you a loan) uses your credit report to decide if you're qualified enough to have that loan. This is a big undertaking for that creditor. If you need $30,000 for a car loan, for example, the creditor has to make sure that you pay your bills on time, because it doesn't want to lend money to someone who has a history of paying back other creditors late.

How does the information get on your credit report? On a monthly basis, the companies and organizations you have done business with report info about you to credit bureaus. There are three major credit bureaus: Experian, Equifax, and TransUnion. So you actually have not one but three credit reports—one from each bureau. Each credit report will be pretty similar, especially for young people who don't have a lengthy credit history. Don't expect a novel when you read your credit report, but if you forgot to pay the minimum balance on your credit card one month, or you stiffed the hospital with medical bills, you can bet they'll be reported.

It's incredibly important to have a strong credit history and a strong credit report. If you ever need a loan for a car or a house, the bank will take this into consideration. And, perhaps more relevant to us, some employers will check your credit report before they hire you. Credit reports show a lot about how responsible you are, and if you don't pay your bills on time, well, a prospective employer might see that as a sign that you won't be a good employee.

Where Do You Check Your Credit Report?

You are entitled to one free credit report each year at AnnualCreditReport.com. This is the only website you should visit to check your credit report. While the aforementioned catchy commercials urging you to check your report are entertaining, their service is, ironically, not free. The website Annual CreditReport.com is issued from the government and is the only trusted source for viewing your credit report.

Once on the site, you can view all three credit reports (again, one from Experian, one from Equifax, and one from TransUnion) at once, or you can choose to view one at a time and space them out over the year. Unless you're about to apply for a car loan or mortgage, it's not that important to check your credit report more than once a year. Just use the freebie yearly to check for mistakes, because they do happen, and if you don't catch them, they can hurt you. See the box below for tips about how to fix them when they do occur.

How Do You Read It?

Once you master the lingo, credit reports are pretty easy to understand. The top of the report shows your name, date of birth, Social Security number, and address. Next it shows what's known as "satisfactory accounts." That includes any current credit cards, the balances owed on them, what the credit limits and minimum payments on the cards are, and the date those accounts were opened. The bottom of the report shows "inquiries." An inquiry is when someone applies for credit. In my case, when I recently checked my Trans-Union report, it showed that I had applied for two different credit cards over the past year. If I had claimed bankruptcy or made late payments on credit cards, these negative items would have been shown on my report too.

Fixing Credit Report Errors

In 2012 the *Columbus Dispatch* ran an article stating that up to 30 percent of credit reports have errors.[1] That's troubling, right?

Let's say you check your credit report and see that the company that granted your car loan claims you were two months late on a payment, but you have proof that you made it on time. The Federal Trade

Commission recommends that you contact both the
credit bureau and the company or organization that
provided the inaccurate info (in this case the
company for your car loan). You should write a letter
(no, not an e-mail) and send it by certified mail to the
credit bureau and the company that made that
mistake. Politely state the error and attach a copy of
the credit report with the error circled. Make the
letter and the documents you attach as easy to
understand as possible for the bureau and the
finance company. You don't want to make this a
crossword puzzle for them. Both sides will
investigate and get back to you as to whether they
think your claim is valid. The process of cleaning up
your credit report may take several months, but that
doesn't mean you should just forget about it. You
don't want to be walking around with inaccurate
information on your record.

What Is a Credit Score and Why Does It Matter?

Remember I said that a credit report is like a high school
transcript? Well, think of your credit *score* as your GPA—the
numerical value that summarizes the info on your credit report. A credit score, just like a credit report, will allow creditors to gauge whether you're a risky customer. Just as a higher
GPA might help you get accepted by more selective colleges,
a higher credit score will make you more attractive to potential lenders and creditors.

You'll not only find it easier to get credit with a high credit
score, but you'll also receive a lower interest rate on your

loans, saving you a lot of money. A low credit score tells the creditor that you're irresponsible with money and that there's a lower chance of you paying a loan back on time. As a result, the creditor needs to charge you a higher interest rate to compensate for that extra risk. No one wants to lend money to someone who's managed money poorly in the past.

Your credit score is determined by a mathematical formula. Dozens of companies have formulas and scoring models, but the model most of the creditors use is from the Fair Isaac Corporation and called the FICO score. We'll stick with this one. You have three FICO scores, one from each of the three credit bureaus. The score from each may differ slightly.

FICO scores range from 300 to 850. Anything over 760 will get you the best (lowest) interest rates on credit cards, mortgages, and loans. Anything below 650, and, well, you're going to have a tough time getting any type of credit, let alone a low interest rate. So how does America stack up? Not too bad. According to the *New York Times*, 53.2 percent of consumers have scores over 700.[2]

It costs money ($19.95) to check your FICO score, and you can do so at myFICO.com. This is the only legitimate place to check your FICO score. Don't fall into the traps set by those commercials!

You don't need to go crazy checking your FICO score all the time. Once a year is adequate, just to check in and see where you stand, though if you're applying for a car loan or mortgage soon, you may want to check it again. If you don't have a good score, you'll want to work on improving it in the months before applying for a car loan or mortgage. We'll discuss what factors affect your FICO score next, so you know what steps you can take to up this important financial stat.

What Determines Your FICO Score?

FICO scores are determined by a number of factors,[3] so let's get familiar with all of them so you can have the highest score possible!

1. Payment History (35 Percent): Your credit card bill arrives in the mail. Ugh. You look at it and immediately regret paying a little extra for first-class airfare to visit your friend in California. In frustration, you throw the bill in your desk drawer, and then, before you know it, you forget to make your payment. Because you didn't pay even a fraction of the bill, this missed payment is going to have a negative impact on your FICO score. Payment history takes into account whether you pay your bills on time, and at 35 percent of your score, it's one of the most important factors in maintaining a high credit score.

2. Amounts Owed (30 Percent): Let's say you went a little wild with your spending this month, and when your credit card bill comes in, you're shocked to see the balance due at $650. You're going to pay your bill, but you can't afford to pay off the whole balance at once and instead opt to make only the minimum payment asked by the credit card company. Not only are you now in credit card debt, but your

FICO score is going to take a hit. Unless you pay off the entire credit card balance each month, your credit score will be affected.

As a simple rule, FICO scores do not take well to credit card debt. Thirty percent of your score is determined by your debt-to-credit-limit ratio or utilization ratio (what you owe over what your available credit line is). A high debt-to-credit ratio lowers your credit score. See the box below for a step-by-step explanation of your utilization ratio.

Computing Your Utilization Ratio

Let's say you have two credit cards: a Visa with a credit limit of $2,000, and an American Express with a credit limit of $4,000. If you owe $1,000 on your Visa and $3,000 on your American Express card, you have $4,000 of credit card debt, with a total credit limit of $6,000 (the $2,000 Visa credit limit plus the $4,000 American Express limit). To figure out your utilization ratio, simply divide the total debt from all your cards by the total credit limit on all your cards. In this case, it would be $4,000 divided by $6,000, which is 66.6 percent. That's a very high utilization ratio. Ideally you want this number to be under 30 percent and as close to zero as possible. A zero utilization ratio means you're not in debt.

---

3. Length of Credit History (15 Percent): Lenders like to see an abundance of available credit. This is why it isn't a good idea to close down credit card accounts, even if there is no balance on them. When you close down a credit card account, you are erasing vital credit history from your report.

Let's say you have three credit cards: one with a $2,000 limit, one with a $4,000 limit, and one with a $3,000 credit limit, totaling $9,000. Let's also say you owe $1,000 on the first card and $3,000 on the second card but nothing on the third card. You're $4,000 in debt, and your debt-to-credit-limit ratio is 44.4 percent. But if you close down that third credit card (the one with a zero balance), you now only have $6,000 of available credit instead of $9,000. You still owe $4,000, so your debt-to-credit-limit ratio ($4,000 ÷ $6,000) skyrockets to 66.6 percent.

If you have credit cards that have no balances on them, but you feel tempted to use them to buy things you don't need, simply cut up the cards rather than close down the accounts.

The actual length of your credit history is out of your control—you can't just push a button and increase your age. Someone who has had a credit card for twenty years will have a longer credit history than a college grad. The longer you have the card, the better your score is, but it's only 15 percent of the score, so don't get too worked up about this.

4. New Credit (10 Percent): You get a credit card offer in the mail and it promises thirty thousand rewards points immediately after you sign up. That sounds great, right? But let's say you signed up for your third card two months ago. If you open this fourth credit card account, your score will drop by a small amount. A potential lender views you signing up for new credit as a sign that you're looking to extend your spending habits. That will make it nervous about lending you money.

5. The Types of Credit You're Using (10 Percent): What kinds of credit do you have and from where? Do you have department or retail store credit cards? Do you have a traditional credit card from a major credit card company? Do you have a mortgage or a car loan?

Don't worry too much about this section of the score. In the next chapter, I'll elaborate on the dangers of department store credit cards (and there are many), but here's how they impact your FICO score: Department store credit cards are very easy to get, so to a creditor it looks as if you are desperate for credit or were denied a traditional credit card because you didn't meet the criteria. It is better for the FICO score if you use a card from the major issuers instead of from a department store. Again, we're not talking about a major impact to your score, but just don't open up tons of store credit card accounts, okay?

To Recap: Your FICO Score Mainly Decreases for These Three Reasons:

1. You pay your bills late (or not at all)
2. You're in credit card debt
3. You close down credit card accounts that you've had for years

How to Raise Your FICO Score

If you know you have a low FICO score, don't sweat it. Just follow the steps below. Yes, it's easier said than done, but a few financial tweaks will result in an increase of your score in a matter of months!

Step 1: Pay your bills on time! It's that simple: never be late. If you can't remember to pay your bills on time, set up reminders through your e-mail or phone.

Step 2: This one's easier said than done. Pay off your credit card balance in full each month. Never make *just* the minimum payment. Pay the entire balance or as close as you can get to it. The idea is to owe nothing, not something!

Step 3: Spend within your means. If you only use your credit card for small purchases, you're bound to stay out of debt. Having a low credit card bill—a $50 bill instead of a $300 bill—makes it easier to pay off the balance in full each month.

Step 4: Don't close down your credit card accounts—you'll eliminate vital credit history. If you no longer wish to use a card, simply cut it up.

Do all this and you're golden!

Insurance and FICO Scores

Did you know that a high credit score could also save you money on car and home insurance rates? There's something known as an Insurance Risk Score (also produced by our friends at FICO), which follows your FICO score. So the higher your FICO score, the higher your Insurance Risk Score will be, and the higher your Insurance Risk Score is, the lower your car/home insurance premiums are.

FICO Score Myths

Now that you know the ins and outs of FICO scores, let's clear up some rumors about them.

Among the many FICO score myths, the notion that checking your score will cause it to decrease tops the list. If you check your credit score or report online, your score will *not* decrease. If a lender, mortgage company, bank, or car dealer checks your credit score, it may have a negative impact, but a pretty minor one (we're only talking about a five-point decrease).

The credit report also does not factor your age, race, occupation, or the state you live in. It's simply a tool creditors use to see if you'll be a responsible customer. Additionally, employ-ers *cannot* check your FICO score, only your credit report.

And that's that! Now you're a FICO score master.

Quick Review

See? Credit isn't as scary or mysterious as you might think. Even if you're not looking to get a car loan or a mortgage anytime soon, don't just throw your hands up and think you don't need to know anything about your credit report or FICO score. It takes years to build up a good credit history, and you want to start working on that now.

Below are the five main points you should remember from this chapter:

1. If you are looking to apply for credit (a car loan, a credit card, or even a mortgage down the road), you need to have a high FICO score and subsequently a clean credit report.
2. Your credit report and FICO score run hand in hand. The info on your credit report makes up your FICO score.
3. Aim to get that FICO score to about 750, since this will get you the lowest interest rates on loans.
4. To raise your FICO and credit scores, pay your bills on time and stay out of debt.
5. You can check your credit report for free by visiting AnnualCreditReport.com, and your FICO score for a fee at myFICO.com.

6

THE CREDIT CARD COMMANDMENTS

All right—finish the following sentence: "There are some things money can't buy. For everything else, there's _____."

Chances are you were able to answer that without skipping a beat. (If you've been living under a rock for the past decade, the missing word is "MasterCard.") This is a powerful example of just how ingrained credit cards have become in our culture.

Aside from this being a textbook case of an advertising campaign that worked, these television spots for MasterCard have put credit cards in a new light—a more lighthearted and likeable one. After seeing these commercials, we start to feel as if credit card companies are our friends. And the credit card companies—like MasterCard, American Express, and Visa—want us to think they're on our side. I wouldn't go so far as saying the credit card companies care about us, but they do provide a valuable service. We definitely *need* credit cards, especially young people starting out.

Why? Because credit cards are the way to build up that ever-coveted FICO score. There's no other way to do it—not with debit cards, not with cash, and not by sitting on your couch watching reruns of *How I Met Your Mother*. You need a credit card to become financially independent, plain and simple.

So what are the best credit cards out there? How can you avoid credit card fees? And how many credit cards should you have? Read on to find out!

The Ins and Outs of Plastic

A credit card allows us to make purchases on credit, meaning you can buy now and pay later. It's not linked to your checking account like a debit card is. Each credit card has a credit limit, which is the maximum amount of money you're allowed to spend on the card. The limit is determined by the credit card company, and could be $500, $1,000, $3,000, or even as high as $20,000. The higher credit limits are generally reserved for customers who have years of credit history. If you're applying for your first credit card, you shouldn't expect a credit limit of more than $1,000.

Credit Cards versus Debit Cards

Sure, they might look the same at first glance, but don't make the amateur error of confusing a credit card with a debit card. With a debit card, you're paying for the item immediately with the money from your checking account. So if you're buying a $30 pair of sunglasses at Sunglass Hut, that $30 leaves your account and goes straight to Sunglass Hut as soon as you swipe your card in the store. With a credit card, you're not using your own money, at least not at the time you buy those shades. Your credit card company is paying for them up front, and then you'll get a bill in about a month, asking you to pay the cost incurred.

Every time you swipe that credit card at a store or use it to buy something online, the retailer has to pay the credit card company a fee, known as an interchange fee (just like with debit cards). So if you buy laundry detergent at Walmart using your MasterCard, Walmart will have to pay a fee to MasterCard. The fees can be up to 6 percent of the purchase price. Remember, you aren't paying this fee, the merchant is, but it's good to know how the process works.

Should You Get a Credit Card?

In short, yes! If you don't have a credit card, get one! There's no reason to be scared about getting a credit card. You just need to know how to use it. For young people like us, credit cards should only be used for small purchases that we can pay back totally when the bill comes. Let me stress this again: if you're going to use a credit card, you need to have the cash to back it up. A lot of people equate credit cards with free money. This can't be further from the truth. Any amount of money you charge on your credit card must be paid back. The credit card trap of swiping and swiping for every last purchase means you'll quickly reach a balance that is more than your budget can allow.

Here Are a Few Examples of Purchases That You Should Put on a Credit Card:

1. Groceries
2. Gas for your car
3. Subway or bus fare
4. Dry cleaning
5. Toiletries

These are all reasonably priced items that are already part of your budget. If you allot $150 for food every month, and you put it on your credit card, you should be able to pay your bill without a problem.

Now, Here Are Some Examples of Purchases That Should Not Be Paid for Using a Credit Card:

1. Vacations
2. Dinner for all your friends
3. Nights at the bar
4. Designer clothes
5. The latest iPhone

The golden rule is this: if you can't pay for it with cash, don't pay for it with your credit card. A vacation in Miami sounds like a fun idea, but unless you have the cash to pay for that trip, you should hold off until you save up a little more money. Otherwise you'll end up paying even *more* for an already expensive purchase. It's just not wise.

Now you may be thinking, well, why even bother with a credit card—why not just cut to the chase and use cash? Cash doesn't prepare you for financial choices later on in life. I know I keep hammering this point home, but having a high FICO score and a great credit report are essential parts of becoming a financially independent adult.

Obviously, though, a credit card can be dangerous if you consistently spend more than you can afford. The best approach is a delicate balance between using your credit card for a few small purchases—perhaps starting off at a limit of $50 a month—and paying for the rest with cash. So no crazy trips to Cabo on AmEx's dime, okay?

How Credit Card Companies Make Money

Credit card companies shouldn't be thought of as benevolent grandparents lending you money whenever you feel like going out to dinner or buying a new coat. They exist to make money. How do they do that? Well, a few ways, but most notably by charging you late fees if you don't pay on time and by charging interest on your purchases if you don't pay off the entire balance each month. And we can't forget another huge source of revenue for the credit card companies: interchange fees, as I mentioned earlier—the one that the merchants pay to the credit card company every time you swipe your card.

The average interest rate on credit cards is 14.92 percent.[1] Is that high? Not as high as it could be. My interest rate is in the low 20s, and that's normal for young cardholders. The higher your interest rate is, the more money it'll cost you if you leave a balance on the card. So if you charge $300 on your credit card, and you don't pay that full amount back by the bill's due date, interest will accrue on the balance. That $300 will turn into $350, $400 . . . There's no limit as to how much the balance can grow. The longer it takes you to pay back the balance, the more the interest will accrue.

Your Credit Card Bill

Here's a sample credit card bill:

Name: Scott Gamm
Account number: xxxxx
Billing period: April 16 to May 15
Transactions:

Sale Date	Description	Amount
4/17	MTA subway	$20
4/19	Amazon.com	$38.25
4/23	Così	$7.94
4/25	WHOLEFDS	$23.71
4/28	Walgreens	$7.63
5/03	Pizza	$7.16
Balance:		$104.69
Minimum payment:		$15.00
Due:		June 10

Every purchase you make using the card is clearly documented, with the date, name of the vendor, and amount. This is a convenient way to track your expenses and create the budget we talked about in the beginning of the book. (Just sayin'!) You'll also see the total balance and the minimum payment that is due. The minimum payment is the amount you *must* pay to avoid a late fee. Each credit card issuer uses a different way to determine the minimum payment. It's usually at least $15–$35 and commonly around 5 percent of your balance. Making only the minimum payment means you're now in debt. In fact, the minimum payment is calculated in a way to *keep you in debt*. If you just make the minimum payment, the remaining balance will accrue interest at whatever rate is attached to your card. So don't get tricked into thinking that paying the minimum payment is a good thing. It's actually a sneaky way to keep you in the hole!

It's easy for me to ask you to pay $105 instead of the more manageable $15. But here is my number one rule of credit card use: if you're going to use your credit card, you *have to pay off the entire balance in full each month*. It's the only way to avoid getting into debt.

If you've made your budget, you probably won't find yourself leaving a balance on your card. But, hey, I know things happen, and it's understandable if one month your budget goes a little haywire and you can't pay off your balance in full. So if you can't afford the entire balance, pay as much as you can. And I mean *as much as you can*—even an extra $5 will make an impact!

Do You Qualify for a Credit Card?

It's not as easy as it used to be for young people to get credit cards, thanks to the Credit CARD Act I mentioned above. This law, which took effect in February 2010, completely reformed the entire credit card industry. Remember when credit card companies would line up on college campuses and hand out free T-shirts to anyone who filled out a credit card application? Well, those days are over!

The Credit CARD Act says that anyone under age twenty-one needs a cosigner on a credit card account, unless they can prove they have sufficient income to make the payments on any potential debt. The law does not specify how much income you need to be exempt from the cosigning rule—it's determined on a case-by-case basis by the credit card issuer. Unless you're rolling in dough, you'll probably need a parent or a relative to cosign on the credit card. The cosigner is totally liable for any debt accrued on the card. If you rack up $1,200 in debt on your credit card and your aunt is the cosigner, well, you're going to have some explaining to do to her, because she's 100 percent responsible for that $1,200—just as you are too. If you are unable to pay that debt, the creditors will knock on your aunt's door and ask her to pay. Your FICO score will be negatively affected and so will your aunt's. So pay up! You don't want any family meltdowns, do you? That'll make for one awkward Thanksgiving.

Other rules of the CARD Act that impacts students are:

1. Credit card companies cannot send preapproved credit card offers to anyone under age twenty-one via mail.

2. Credit card companies must stay a thousand feet away from college campuses when trying to solicit/market cards to students.
3. Creditors can no longer give out an incentive (free T-shirt, free lunch) to students if they apply for a credit card.

Preapproved Credit Card Offers

We just threw around the word "preapproved" when talking about the CARD Act and credit card applications. So here's what that means: You might be surprised to hear that a preapproved credit card offer is not that different from a regular credit card offer. The term "preapproved" is a marketing tactic used to lure customers. Basically, credit card companies do some research and determine a select group of consumers whom they feel have the best chance of being approved for the credit card—this way, the company doesn't have to waste money by sending offers to people who have no chance of being approved. Receiving a preapproved credit card offer, ironically, does not guarantee that you'll be approved for the card. You still have to go through the application process. Stay tuned, though, because we're about to talk about the process of signing up for a credit card.

If you're over twenty-one, you won't need a cosigner, but you still might run into some hurdles. If it's your first credit card, it's riskier for the credit card company to take you on as a customer, because you have no financial track record (yet to get that financial track record you need a credit card, so it is rather ironic).

Want to know what types of cards you should apply for? Keep reading!

What Type of Card Should I Get?

Your first credit card doesn't have to be some fancy card that's gold or platinum and has a robust rewards program that gives you free plane tickets to Paris every year (although that would be nice). Save that for later in life when you can use your card for big purchases without breaking a sweat. Here are a few types of credit cards that are available to young people just starting out in the financial world:

1. Secured Credit Card

A secured credit card is great regardless of whether you are over or under twenty-one. To use a secured credit card, you must make a security deposit of a few hundred dollars. This security deposit acts as the credit limit. If I deposit $300 to the card, that's the maximum amount of money I can spend. If I start going crazy shopping at J. Crew and charge up a $300 balance, and fail to pay that $300, the credit card company will take my security deposit as collateral. It's just like a security deposit when renting an apartment: if you trash the place, well, good luck getting your money back when you move out.

Beware of the relatively high fees associated with secured

credit cards, so shop around to find the best one by doing a Google search.

The goal of having a secured credit card is to eventually be approved for a traditional line of credit (your more standard card that doesn't require a security deposit). In order to accomplish this goal, use the card responsibly. Even one mistake can throw you off course. Here are some tips:

- Did I mention that it's important to pay off the balance in full and on time? Let me reiterate this again: *pay it in full!*
- Never approach or exceed your credit limit.
- After one or two years of responsibly using a secured credit card, you'll be able to apply for and receive a traditional credit card (like AmEx, MasterCard, etc.) with a larger credit limit and perhaps even a robust rewards program. You can apply for a traditional credit card from the same company that issued your secured card, or, now that you've established some sort of a credit record, you can try your luck at applying for a card from a different company. The choice, my friends, is yours!

2. Department Store Credit Cards

We've all been there: you're shopping at Target, and the cashier asks, "Would you like to get a store credit card and get a 10 percent discount every time you shop?" Tempting, isn't it? Let me warn you, it's not a good idea! Here's why:

1. Interest Rates: Interest rates on department store credit cards are rather high, much higher than a traditional credit card from a creditor like American Express or Visa. For example, a Bloomingdale's credit card has an interest rate of around 24.5 percent (the rate is variable, meaning it fluctuates). A credit card from Kohl's has an interest rate of 21.9 percent, but that rate will jump to 24.9 percent if you make a late payment. So if you buy a $200 dress or a $200 suit and get a 15 percent discount using your store card, but then you don't pay off the balance in full and the 22 percent interest kicks in, you're actually now paying 3.7 percent more for the item than you would have if you had used cash. That doesn't make financial sense!

2. Urge to Shop: Let's say you get a credit card from a department store you love to shop at (hmmm . . . Macy's? Bloomingdale's?) and, as a result, every time you use the card at the store, you receive a 15 percent discount. That sounds great at first, but really it's just the store cultivating your urge to shop. This discount may give you an excuse to buy unnecessary items in that store. It's called "wandering eye" shopping. "That leather jacket looks nice. Yeah it's $500, but with my Macy's credit card, I'll get a 15 percent discount." Nope! Put the jacket down and get the hell out of the store—you're not buying it! Tough!

3. Your FICO Score: As I mentioned in the last chapter, department store credit cards are generally looked down upon from FICO's point of view. Enough said.

3. Traditional Credit Cards

If you can find a parent or relative who is willing to cosign on the card (no bribing allowed!) and you're over twenty-one, then go ahead and apply for a traditional card from a creditor like Capital One, Visa, or MasterCard. Be aware of the interest rate: it is variable, meaning it can change at any time. You'll rarely find a credit card with a fixed interest rate that you can just lock in and not have to think about.

4. Credit Union Cards

Remember we talked about credit unions in chapter 2? In addition to checking and savings accounts, credit unions also offer credit cards, with the following perks you may not get from the land of American Express or Visa:

1. Better Rates: Credit unions usually have lower interest rates on their credit cards. Remember, credit unions are nonprofit, and, unlike regular credit card companies, don't waste money on lobbying or high executive bonuses. Credit unions use that savings to offer more attractive products to its members. Why should you care about a lower interest rate on a credit card? If you leave a balance on the card and the interest kicks in, well, it's better to have a lower rate than a higher one—since that means you'll be charged less interest, and thereby, owe less money But, since you're following all of the advice in this book to a tee, you'll be paying off your balance in full each month, right?

2. Fewer Fees: If you get a traditional credit card, I bet you'll soon feel sick and tired of the endless fees the major companies charge. Don't be surprised to find that most credit unions have very few fees, if any.

3. It's Personal: Since credit unions are smaller and formed by members only, it is not uncommon for members to receive face-to-face time with credit union representatives to ensure that each member clearly understands the terms of their credit card. You're treated as a valued member of the credit union, as opposed to just another customer, like at a bank.

Authorized User

Another way to build credit at a young age is to become an authorized user on your parent's (or relative's) credit card. You are essentially a guest on their card. Just make sure your parent (or whoever is the card's primary user) has *stellar* credit. In a process known as "piggybacking," your credit score will improve if you are an authorized user on a card owned by someone with strong credit.

Piggybacking has become increasingly unpopular and may even be prohibited by the credit bureaus within the near future. It is not the ideal method. Stick to the various options mentioned earlier (secured cards, a cosigner, credit unions). I think it's important to go through the process of signing up for a credit card and doing everything on your own rather than having to rely on mom and dad.

The Process of Signing up for a Credit Card

How do you go about getting a card? If you're over twenty-one, you may receive credit card offers in the mail. Some will tell you you're "preapproved," but a preapproved credit card offer is not that different from a regular credit card offer, as mentioned before.

Applying online for a credit card is the best and most stress-free option, as opposed to filling out one of those silly credit card offers you may have received in the mail. Just visit each credit card company's website to see what credit cards they offer. It's that simple.

And now you must be asking—well, there are so many—which one should I choose?

There's no magic answer, but know this: do not choose a credit card with an annual fee. This is a stupid fee where you are literally paying money to use the credit card. Some credit cards waive the annual fee for the first year, but then you have to pay it every year after that. But there are plenty of credit cards with no annual fee ever. So just Google "no annual fee credit cards."

When tackling the application, you'll need your basic information on hand, like your Social Security number and your annual income, and you may even need to disclose how much money you have in a savings, checking, or retirement account. Chances are, the application process will only take a few minutes, but you'll have to wait a bit longer for the results. You'll receive either an e-mail or a letter in the mail from the credit card company telling you whether you've been approved for the card. If you've been approved, you should receive the card via mail in a few weeks. It's that easy. If you are rejected, it means the credit card company views you as a risky client, either because you have a low FICO score or no FICO score at all. Don't get discouraged if you are rejected. Young people don't have extensive credit histories, so it may take a few tries. Try applying for a card from another issuer or look into a secured credit card. You'll get one eventually!

How Many Credit Cards Should You Have?

Should you have one card, two, ten, or thirty? Think I'm a bit crazy to throw such high figures around? I thought I was too, until I read a recent Reuters.com article that profiled a man with forty credit cards (yes, you read that correctly)![2] His rationale for having so many cards, the article suggests, is that he can earn tons of rewards points. Obviously, I would not recommend that approach.

Here's another crazy stat: 50 percent of college students have four or more credit cards, according to Sallie Mae.[3] If you're in college, you should have only *one* credit card. You don't yet have an income to support your purchases, so there's no reason to be applying for every credit card under the sun. You should only be using the card for small purchases. If you're just out of college and have a steady income, it's okay to have two or three.

Paying Late: It's a Problem

This is a true story: when I was in the midst of writing this chapter on credit cards, I realized that I forgot to pay my credit card bill. Now, normally I'm responsible, with reminders set to go off on the tenth of the month to let me know that if I haven't paid my bill already, it's time to log on and do it. But this time I got distracted by writing, going on Facebook, talking to my sisters on the phone, and before I knew it, it was ten after five. I scrambled to get online to make the payment, but it was too late. Right at the bottom of the screen, by the Authorize Payment button, there's a notice stating that if the company hasn't received your monthly payment by 5:00 p.m. on its due date, it won't be processed until the next day.

By now, readers, you probably have guessed that I didn't just sit idly by and let the late fee and interest charges ruin my day and my wallet. I was only ten minutes late, after all! So I decided to call up the credit card issuer and ask the rep to avoid charging me the late fee and any interest (remember my interest rate on this card is just over 20 percent—and that's high). Shockingly, it worked. The rep added a notation to my account to say that this payment would be considered on time and no late fee or interest charges would apply. Phew!

If I hadn't taken the initiative and pleaded my case to the credit card company's representative, what would have happened? I would've been charged a $25 late fee plus interest charges, but that's not the worst of it. If you are even a single day late, the company can raise the interest rate on your card. Just like that! My interest rate is 20 percent, and if I pay late, they can raise it to 29.99 percent (and this information is dis-closed—so check your statement to see what level they can raise your interest rate to if you pay late). Wow! Now *that's* something I want to avoid. Paying one day late generally won't have a (huge) impact on your FICO score, but being thirty to ninety days late will knock the score down.

The moral of the story? Pay on time. Create an alert on your cell phone to remind you to pay on time. Or write it on your hand—whatever you have to do to prevent you from for-getting to pay your credit card bill. I got lucky when the com-passionate customer service lady waived my fee and eventually waived the interest charges. I might not be so lucky next time, so why risk it?

If Your Credit Card Is Stolen

In chapter 2 we talked about who is liable when your debit card is stolen, but what happens if someone steals your credit card and starts charging up stuff left and right? Will you have to pay for the MacBook Air some criminal picked up under your name? Thankfully, the answer is no. According to the Federal Trade Commission, you're only liable for a maximum of $50 if a thief uses the card before you report it stolen.[4] So even if they go on a shopping spree at the Apple Store, it won't affect you very much, if at all. If only the credit card number is stolen, and not the actual card, you won't owe anything.

If you lose your card or fear the card was stolen, be smart and call the credit card company immediately.

The Downside of Credit Cards

You've heard some pretty great things about credit cards so far: how they can help you build credit and how they can help you track your expenses. But of course there are some downsides to using them too.

Credit Card Fees and How to Avoid Them

Don't be surprised if you get nailed with credit card fees. They're a key way that credit card companies make money off their customers. Here are some of the most common fees:

1. Late Fees: When you make a late payment, you'll be charged a fee that could be higher than your minimum payment. As stated in the Credit CARD Act, the maximum late fee a credit card company can charge is $25 if you are a customer who has consistently paid your bill on time. If you rarely pay on time, you will be charged late fees that are higher than that. If you pay late twice during six billing periods, a $35 late fee will apply. I don't need to tell you again, but I will anyway: pay your bill on time!

2. Activity Fees: The Credit CARD Act banned inactivity fees, which are fees charged if you don't use your credit card. But do you think a ban on inactivity fees would scare credit card companies? Of course not! Now there are "activity fees," which occur if you don't charge up a certain amount on your card. They're pretty uncommon, but they do exist. In some cases, the fee, which can be more than $50, is refunded once your charges exceed the limit set by the credit card company.

3. Over-the-Limit Fees: If your credit card limit is $500 and you purchase $515 worth of clothing, you'll be charged a fee because you exceeded your credit limit. Never approach or go over your credit limit (remember, stick to small purchases under $50 per month and you'll be in a better position to stay out of debt).

4. Rewards Redemption Fees: Got airline miles and want to redeem them? Not so fast! Credit card companies may charge a fee if you want to use the points or miles you worked so hard to accumulate over the years, and they can be around $30–$50.

5. Paper Statement Fees: If you want statements mailed to your home each month, you gotta pay up! To avoid this fee, ask the credit card company to stop mailing you statements, and check out your statements for free online.

6. Currency Conversion Fees: If you're going abroad, you should be aware of what's known as a currency conversion fee (usually 2–3 percent of the purchase). A currency conversion fee is charged anytime you use your credit card or withdraw money from your bank account while abroad. Credit card companies charge this because the American currency has to be converted to the currency of the country you're visiting for the purchase to be completed. Various

Capital One, Discover, and American Express credit cards do not charge a currency conversion fee, making them the best bet for you if you plan to spend a lot of time abroad.

Why Credit Cards Make You Spend Money

Let's say you're strolling around the mall and see a pair of sneakers on sale for $40. You've been in the market for a new pair for a while and decide to buy them. At the register, the total comes up, and you have to decide: cash or credit?

If you have $50 in your wallet and you buy a $40 pair of shoes using cash, you're depleting a staggering 80 percent of your cash supply. Shelling out two $20 bills literally feels like you're removing a lot of stuff from your wallet, right? Meanwhile, if you use a credit card to pay for the shoes, with a quick and easy swipe you're able to walk out of the store with those shoes and the $50 still in your wallet. Instead of the depleted feeling you get when you hand over cash, you barely notice how much you spent.

Research backs this up. A study led by NYU Stern marketing professor Priya Raghubir set out to determine what effect credit cards have on our spending. And it had some very interesting results: the study suggested that "less transparent payment forms [such as credit cards] tend to be treated like [play] money and are hence more easily spent (or parted with)."[5]

Play money! Can you believe that?

When you have a credit card, it's important to keep yourself in check. The next time you're looking at your statement, if you notice a bunch of frivolous, crazy expenditures, maybe it's a sign that you should be on a cash diet for a while. Remember, a credit card shouldn't be treated like Monopoly money.

How Credit Card Companies Woo You

To encourage you to keep swiping that card, most credit cards come with a rewards program: airline miles, points for hotels, electronics, cruises. Chances are, your first credit card won't have a rewards program (or if it does, it will be something minor, like 1 or 2 percent cash back on all your purchases). Rewards programs sound great, but as a young credit card user, they shouldn't factor into your spending decisions. The goal of a credit card is to be able to show the credit bureaus that you're responsible with money, not to spend so much that you accumulate rewards points toward a free flight to Barcelona.

Why Credit Card Companies Don't Care about Young People

In 2009 credit card companies spent over $83 million to market and promote student credit cards, according to the Federal Reserve. As a result of those marketing efforts, credit card issuers gained an additional fifty-three thousand student credit card accounts.[6] In 2010 the amount charged by students dropped 13 percent, to $73,261,906 (a decrease of $11,200,859). But just because students charged less doesn't mean the credit card companies weren't still roping in tons of young customers.

Credit card companies are notorious for marketing specifically toward students. While the aforementioned Credit CARD Act banned companies from giving students incentives if they sign up for a card and prohibited companies from setting up marketing tents within a thousand feet of campus, that doesn't mean they're invisible. I saw a credit card company giving out iced tea and popcorn outside a bank located about one block from a dorm at school. You didn't need to sign up for a credit card to receive the goodies (thus following the CARD Act), but it was still trying to lure students into the branch.

Bottom line? Stay away from marketing tents on or near college campuses. Credit cards offered at these tents typically come with hidden fees and high interest rates. Finding the best credit card requires some research and strategy, as mentioned at the beginning of the chapter.

How the Credit CARD Act Has Failed to Protect Students

In my opinion, the measures put forth by the Credit CARD Act are not strict enough. The intentions behind the plan are good, but there are plenty of loopholes that allows banks to prey on students. Just take the case of the bank setting up its tent by the NYU dorm. It wasn't breaking the rules, but it was certainly trying to sway students.

The Credit CARD Act also prohibits credit card companies from mailing preapproved credit card offers to anyone under twenty-one, as we mentioned earlier in this chapter. They are still permitted to send traditional credit card offers though, and they do. According to Jim Hawkins, professor at the University of Houston, 76 percent of students said they had received a credit card offer in the mail since the start of 2010.[7] I know I'm just one guy in a sea of credit card users, but in my humble opinion the legislation should have banned *all* types of credit card offers from being sent to those under the age of twenty-one.

And credit card companies are always looking for new ways to exploit their customer base. A March 2012 article on WSJ.com showed how the major credit card companies are targeting young people on social media outlets like Twitter, Facebook, and Foursquare.[8] They'll post a barrage of tweets and Facebook status updates or offer game-based incentives in the hopes that people will "like" a credit card company's Facebook page. The article mentions how American Express is using this tactic the most, though a spokeswoman for AmEx claims the social media campaign isn't targeted to "undergrads or anyone under the age of 21."[9] A violation of the Credit CARD Act? Absolutely not. The laws didn't mention social media. In fact, when the law was written, in 2008–9, social media wasn't as popular as it is today. So it's a little sneaky.

Bottom line? Let's not rely on the government to solve our credit woes—it's called personal responsibility!

When it comes down to it, don't be blinded by the glitz and glamour of credit card campaigns. Like I said at the beginning of the chapter, credit card companies will try to pull on your heartstrings or fill your head with dreams of trips around the world, but when boiled down to its essence, a credit card company is a business. Choose the business you want to deal with wisely, and you'll reap the rewards.

Quick Review

Whew! After all that, you should be a master of plastic. Here are the most important points to remember:

1. A credit card is not an ATM. It is a tool that enables you to build a strong credit score.
2. Only use your credit card for small purchases—no more than $50 a month to start—so you can be sure to pay the balance every month.
3. Do I sound like a broken record yet? Pay your credit card balance in full each month! If you are over your budget and can't pay it all off, pay as much as possible.
4. Never pay just the minimum—it's been calculated to keep you in debt.
5. Be wary of sneaky fees that are sometimes attached to credit cards.

7

DEBT IS A BITCH

Here's the scene: Me, walking out of class. The look on my face can be described as somewhere between mystified and horrified. I'm listening to my friend describe how he dropped $1,000 in a matter of minutes on a $700 briefcase and a new pair of $300 dress shoes. Why was my friend suddenly spending insane amounts of money on these items? Because he just found out that he was hired for a summer internship. An *unpaid* summer internship.

Did my friend have $1,000 to shell out for these items? Of course not! But since his credit card had a limit of $2,000, it didn't seem like an issue to him to charge up $1,000. After all, he's about to embark on a summer internship on Wall Street, and even interns have to look good, right?

As you can imagine, those purchases were not paid off in full when the credit card bill came. It took my friend a year to pay off that debt, plus the interest charges, which came to more than $100, thanks to the double-digit interest rate on his credit card.

While this story may sound like an extreme case (and I wish it was), the average credit card debt being carried by students is about $3,100, according to Sallie Mae.[1] Thankfully, the median credit card debt levels for Americans dropped 7.8 percent during the recession and the average credit card debt fell, between 2007 and 2010, to $7,100, according to the Federal Reserve.[2]

It's easy to get into credit card debt. Perhaps you fell prey to the "swiping without thinking" trap we discussed in the last chapter. Or maybe you had no choice but to get into debt, because you lost a job and needed to use your credit card to finance basic necessities like groceries.

Regardless of how you got into debt, there are plenty of ways to get out of it. Trust me—you don't have to be treading water in a sea of credit card debt forever.

The Debt Trap

Let's start off on an obvious note: being in credit card debt is not a situation you want to find yourself in. That's why I've been hammering home the point that you should pay off your credit card bill in full. There are serious consequences that come from being in debt—physically, mentally, and emotionally.

We talked, in chapter 5, about how debt negatively impacts your FICO score, but your financial health is only one facet of the debt disease. The United Kingdom's Consumer Credit Counselling Service did a study in which 66 percent of the participants said debt hindered their performance at work.[3] It makes sense. Worrying about debt can keep you up at night, making you less effective during the daily grind. The study also showed that the stress from being in debt often hurts personal relationships.

Credit card debt, especially among students, poses health problems. A 2007 study of ten thousand college students from various campuses in Minnesota showed that "students with more than $1,000 in credit card debt reported higher rates of depression, worked more hours and gambled more."[4] Another 2007 study by Arizona State University's Health and Wellness Center showed that students with "high-risk credit behavior" were more likely to use cigarettes, cocaine, and amphetamines and were less likely to wear a seat belt.[5] The study also revealed how credit card debt resulted in more cases of sadness and exhaustion among students.

Debt certainly isn't the type of issue you can just try to forget about or hope it will disappear. It won't. Facing your debt head on is the only way out!

How Do You Stack Up?

Okay, so what are the balances on your credit cards? What are the interest rates? I don't mean to sound cynical, but my guess is that most people aren't able to answer these questions with anything better than a ballpark estimate. And if you want a clean financial slate, there's no room for guesswork. It's like trying to get your cholesterol lower without having a blood test to see what your cholesterol level is!

Before you try to clean up your financial life, take a quick look through your credit card statements to gauge where you are. You may owe money on more than one credit card, which makes this debt-free quest a bit more complicated.

Here's a chart to help you realize your debt. (Go ahead, fill it in right now!) Write the name of the card in the first column, followed by the interest rate, balance you owe, and minimum payment for each card. All of this info can be found on your credit card statement.

Card Name (Visa, AmEx, etc.)	Interest Rate	Debt/ Balance	Minimum Payment

Add up the third column (the debt/balance column) and that's how much credit card debt you have in total.

Now fill in the blank:

I have $_____ in credit card debt, and I'm proud of it!

That's right! You're proud because you're about to embark on a mission to crush that number to smithereens—ready?

Get That Interest Rate Lowered

Let me reiterate—if you leave a balance on the credit card, the interest will accrue. You don't have to worry about interest if you pay your entire credit card balance off in full each month. So if you do leave a balance on the credit card, that means you're in debt. Now, the reason your credit card debt is constantly increasing is due to the high interest rate on your cards. You already know that high interest rates are one of the primary ways that credit card companies make money, so you need to combat that interest as best you can to try to climb out of this debt. Getting a lower interest rate—even 15 percent instead of 20 percent—will be incredibly helpful to you on this journey.

Let's use a hypothetical example to show how even a small change in interest rate will save you money. Say Robert owes $1,600 on his Visa card at a 23 percent interest rate. Robert is responsible for paying off the entire $1,600 balance (the principal), and he's also on the hook for the interest that accumulates over time. The longer it takes Robert to pay off that $1,600, the more interest will accrue. With a 23 percent interest rate, Robert's minimum monthly payment will be just under $50. What if he could get that interest rate knocked down to 10 percent? The minimum payment would drop to a mere $30! That's *much* more manageable and appealing, if you ask me.

The good news is that in real life it's not very hard to get your interest rates lowered. The most effective way is to do what's called a "balance transfer." And you do it in a seemingly counterintuitive way—by opening up a new credit card account. Not just any old credit card, however. You need one that's going to help you in this battle! Here's how: do a quick Google search for "balance transfer card" and apply online for one. It doesn't matter if it's with the same credit card company or a different one—what matters is that these cards typically have a zero percent promotional interest rate. That zero percent promotional rate is key—it means you pay no interest for at least a year (it could even be eighteen months, depending on the duration of the promotion). If the card doesn't have a zero percent promotional rate for at least a year, search for a different one. Once you've found the right one and have applied and been approved, the balance from your original card will be transferred to this new credit card.

Getting Rejected for a Balance Transfer Card

You may not get approved for a balance transfer card right away. They are typically subject to credit checks, and if you have high debt levels, chances are your FICO score isn't too good. If you don't get approved, apply for one or two other balance transfer cards from different credit card issuers. If nobody accepts you, keep on reading, because I'm going to share a few more effective ways to get out of debt!

So if our pal Robert transfers his entire $1,600 balance to a zero percent card, his minimum payment will drop from $50 to around $15 a month. Robert will save $370 in interest charges over the course of the promotion (in this case twelve months) because he is now paying zero percent interest on his debt, as compared to 23 percent on his original card.

As always, there is a catch (you were expecting one, right?). Some balance transfer cards charge a fee to transfer the balance, usually around 4 percent of the balance you want to transfer. In Robert's case, that would be a fee of $64. Now, when we just calculated Robert's case, we assumed no balance transfer fee. Given his situation, it's still worth paying the fee, since he'll still be saving over $300 by doing this. But there are tons of balance transfer cards out there with *no balance transfer fee*. All you have to do is Google "no-fee balance transfer cards." Some of these fee-free balance transfer cards require you to transfer the debt within thirty days of opening the account, but you're so on top of your game that you won't have a problem getting that done.

Once you have this balance transfer card, you have some work to do to take advantage of the zero percent interest rate. When the zero percent rate expires after a year or a year and a half, the card switches to a much higher interest rate, often around 20 percent, so you need to hustle to pay off this debt. You're going to have to scrimp and save and gather any extra money you can during the small window when you're paying no interest.

Don't use the new balance transfer card to make small purchases, like your groceries or a new shower curtain, as you would with a normal credit card. The zero percent interest rate, in most cases, only applies to the debt you're transferring. If you use the card for purchases and you don't pay those purchases off in full, well, that balance will be charged at the card's regular interest rate. If you think you might be tempted to spend on the balance transfer card, don't be afraid to cut up the card to prevent you from using it. (Don't throw it away, though, because you may need to access the credit card number at some point. I learned this the hard way!)

If you owe money on the card by the time the promotional rate expires, you can always transfer that balance to another balance transfer card with a zero percent rate. But at some point, you have to start paying, because constantly transferring the balance only kicks the can down the road (like what our government does with the debt crisis facing the country!). It doesn't fix your main problem.

Balance Transfer Cards and FICO

Earlier I noted how opening up several credit card accounts within a short period of time could hurt your FICO score. If you're concerned about getting a balance transfer card for that reason, here's my response: are you kidding? That's like saying, "My car got totaled, but I'm most upset that a bird pooped on it." Your credit card debt is the most pressing issue, not the fact that you're getting another credit card.

Always Pay More Than the Minimum

Regardless of whether you opted for a balance transfer, paying more than the monthly minimum is the number one rule when it comes to paying off credit cards. It will get you out of debt quicker, and you'll accumulate less interest.

Credit card companies actively set minimum payments to keep you in debt, which is why Congress touched upon this issue in the epic Credit CARD Act. Thanks to the legislation, credit card companies now must clearly show on your credit card statement exactly how much in interest you'll be charged and how long it will take you to get out of debt if you only pay the minimum. And the numbers are scary.

If our friend Robert only pays the $50 minimum on his $1,600 balance, it'll take him over fourteen years to pay off that debt, and he'll pay almost $2,500 in interest in addition to paying off the $1,600 principal! Isn't that crazy? His $1,600 debt turned into over $4,000! By making the minimum payment of $50 a month, Robert may think he's eating away at his $1,600 balance, but he's really not doing anything to eliminate his debt.

Here's a pretty interesting rule of thumb. Generally speaking, no matter how much debt you have, if you can pay double the minimum each month, you'll be out of debt in about two years. If Robert can pay $100 a month toward his credit card debt, instead of the minimum of $50, he'll be out of debt in just under two years, and he'll only pay about $350 in interest, as compared to almost $2,500 if he sticks with making only the minimum payment.

Now, you may be thinking, well, Scott, that's easy for you to say, but how am I going to find the extra money to pay more than the minimum payment? Well, by following the tips in chapters 3 and 4! Whether you become a king of coupons, the master of home-cooked meals, or the most competitive bargain shopper on the planet, finding creative ways to save money isn't as hard as you may think. The money you save by not going out every weekend or by not buying lunch every day can then be applied to your debt. Even $5 or $10 more than the minimum payment will make a bigger dent than you think!

Contacting Your Credit Card Company

Calling up your credit card company and asking for a lower interest rate is a bit risky. It could backfire on you: the credit card company may view this as a sign of weakness and, in response, close your account or drop your credit limit. Lowering your credit limit raises your utilization ratio and closing down a credit card account will erase vital credit history from your credit report. You remember this from the last chapter, right!? (Psst . . . It's on page 81 in case you need a refresher!)

If you do have the guts to call up the credit card company and ask for a lower rate, make sure you come armed with the fact that you've been a good customer in the past. And while this might sound sneaky, don't act like you're in financial hardship, even if it's true. If this is your first time in credit card debt, tell them that. If you've been a loyal customer for years and have always paid on time, let them know. You have to give yourself the best shot, and to

do that you'll need to present the best possible profile
of yourself.

Focus on the Card with the Highest Interest Rate

What if you have credit card debt on several cards? It's obviously not as simple as navigating debt on a single card, but it's
possible to climb out of this hole by following the plan I'll lay
out for you next.

Let's say you have three credit cards with debt on them:

1. Visa, with a $1,000 balance, 25 percent interest rate,
   and minimum monthly payment of $30
2. MasterCard, with a $800 balance, 12 percent interest
   rate, and minimum monthly payment of $16
3. American Express, with a $400 balance, 18 percent in-
   terest rate, and minimum monthly payment of $15

Which one should you start paying off first? If you
guessed Visa, you're right. The one with the highest interest
rate is the one you should pay first, because it is the card that's
costing you the most money. Even if the highest balance isn't
on the card with the highest interest rate, you still want to
start with that card.

Let's get down to the nitty-gritty. Here's how to tackle
this debt:

Step 1: Cut up all your credit cards except for one, to be
kept for emergencies only. If you're serious about paying off

debt, you need to stop using your credit cards entirely. Remember, don't close down the credit card account, since that will hurt your FICO score.

Step 2: Your main priority right off the bat is that Visa card with the sky-high interest rate. This card has a monthly minimum payment of $30. You're going to try and pay double that, or $60 a month instead. If you can pay more than that, great. Find any extra cash, even if you have to sell some old clothes, DVDs, or the three pairs of shoes you bought over the summer (you know who you are!).

While you're focusing on the Visa card, you need to continue to make the minimum payments on the other two cards (the MasterCard and American Express). Why? Because we're not focused on these two cards yet, so we're just going to let them tread water. But if you ignore the other two cards and fail to make the minimum payments, you'll get slammed with late fees and the damage to your FICO score will be even more severe.

Step 3: Once the Visa card is paid off, you're going to take that $60 a month you were putting toward it and direct it to the card with the next highest interest rate, in this case the American Express. The American Express account has a minimum payment of $15, and by paying $60 instead you'll be paying four times the minimum, crushing your debt levels.

While you're paying off the American Express, you'll still make the minimum payment on the last credit card, the MasterCard.

Step 4: Once the American Express card is paid off, you'll again take that $60 and direct it toward the MasterCard. Once again you'll be paying almost four times the minimum. Now, if you really want to be ambitious, since all along you were paying the original $16 minimum toward this card while focusing on the other two cards, you can essentially afford to pay $75 toward this MasterCard.

If you happen to have more than three credit cards, simply continue this process until all the cards are paid off.

Step 5: Celebrate—okay, maybe you can now buy back some of the DVDs you sold to get out of debt, but not all of them. You're now debt-free.

Don't get me wrong—this process doesn't happen overnight. Depending on how much money you can scrape up to direct toward these cards, it could take a year or it could take three years. The more money you throw at this debt, the faster the debt will disappear.

Debt Management Plans

The strategies I mentioned above work best for debt under $15,000. If you have credit card debt that is higher than that, you may need to consider some stronger remedies.

One of those remedies is enrolling in a debt management plan from a credit counselor. The National Foundation for Credit Counseling is a nonprofit organization that can refer you to a reputable credit counselor in your area. A credit counselor is a qualified professional who can enroll you in a debt management plan that aims to make you debt-free within three to five years.

The fees for a credit counselor are relatively low—they vary by state but shouldn't be more than $50 a month. And if you can't afford the fees, let the counselor know and he or she may drop the fees.

Under a debt management plan, your credit card is frozen to stop you from doing any additional spending. The credit counselor's main role is to talk with the credit card company on your behalf and ask it to lower the interest rates on the cards. Together, the counselor and the credit card company determine a monthly payment plan for you. You make payments to the counselor, who passes the money along to the credit card company. The counselor will even help prevent debt collectors from calling your house and late fees from being charged.

I like debt management plans because the counselor guides you and does most of the dirty work (like negotiating with the credit card companies). I would only use one, though, if your debt level has crept up into five digits. If your debt is under $10,000, stick with the basic strategies I talked about at the beginning of the chapter (balance transfers, paying more than the minimum payment). The debt management plan is a three to five year program, whereas if you were to tackle this on your own, you could be out of debt in as little as two years, depending on how much money you can gather.

Debt Management Plans versus Debt Settlement Companies

Don't confuse debt management plans with debt settlement companies. Debt settlement companies, in my opinion, are a complete mess. They're out to turn a profit, and let's put it this way: you don't need to make someone else (aside from the credit card company) rich off your debt.

Bankruptcy

Being in debt can feel like you're sinking in quicksand. If your debt is out of control—I'm talking about being in more debt than you can imagine, like over $50,000—bankruptcy could be the best solution. Yes, I know, "bankruptcy" is a scary word, but in certain cases it's a smart decision.

Bankruptcy is a legal proceeding, which is facilitated in court. You'll really need a bankruptcy attorney to guide you through the process. Here are the two types of bankruptcies you want to familiarize yourself with:

1. Chapter 7: This is where all or most of your debts are erased. We're talking about credit card debt or medical bills, not student loan debt (more on student loans in the next chapter).

> Chapter 7 bankruptcy protection means you have to give up your assets, like a car or your home. Chances are you don't own a home yet, so for young people, claiming Chapter 7 usually means having to give up a car if they have one.

> Each state has slightly different laws when it comes to Chapter 7, which is why it's best to talk to an attorney when considering this type of bankruptcy.

2. Chapter 11: This type of bankruptcy is probably more sensible than Chapter 7 for young people. With Chapter 11, you have to pay back your debts within three to five years, but you can keep your assets.

Bankruptcy will remain on your credit report for up to ten years, making it extremely difficult to get a car loan or a mortgage. Hopefully, you will never find yourself in a situation where you need to claim bankruptcy. It's a last resort and, again, only for extremely high debt levels.

Quick Review

Bet you're ready to destroy your debt now! Here are the key points to remember:

1. Try to transfer your credit card balances to a credit card with a zero percent promotional rate. This will save you tons of money in interest costs.
2. Try to make at least twice the minimum payment, but if that's not possible, put as much as you can toward it. Even an extra $5 or $10 will help!
3. If you have debt on more than one credit card, start focusing on the card with the highest interest rate first, since that's the card costing you the most money.
4. For extremely high levels of credit card debt, you might need to consider a debt management plan or even bankruptcy.

8

PAYING FOR COLLEGE

I became aware of the high cost of tuition when I was in middle school, thanks to having two older sisters who were in college. And it scared me. Given my family's financial struggles, I knew I needed to help pay for my future tuition in some way, whether by earning some money to put toward future college expenses or by maintaining good grades to increase my chances for scholarships. By the time I got to college, thanks to working throughout high school, the money I made from my website, and a savings fund that was put into place when I was in elementary school, the burden of paying for college wasn't as bad as it could have been. But it still hasn't been easy.

As college costs rise each year at levels that seem beyond control, student loans are becoming more and more popular. The College Board estimates that from 2001 to 2002 and 2011 to 2012, tuition costs for public state schools has risen by 5.6 percent more than the rate of inflation each year.[1] From 2008 to 2010, the average tuition at a four-year public college rose 15 percent, according to a *Washington Post* article.[2] For private schools, the increase has been smaller but still 2.6 percent more than the rate of inflation.[3] In this day and age, most people aren't able to pull tuition costs out of their pocket.

Whether you're about to head off to college or grad school, you're in college, or you've just graduated and are worried about how to repay your student loans, this chapter is going to put your doubts to rest.

Choosing the Right College

This is a very tough topic to write about. No one can tell you where to go to school. It's a personal decision.

When I was in high school, I was totally lost during the college-application process. I knew I wanted to study business, but the best undergraduate business schools were all private institutions with tuition costs well above $40,000 a year. I decided to apply to a number of different business schools, both public and private. I was accepted into a state business school and at NYU's Stern School of Business. Both were great schools, but—I'm not going to try and sugarcoat the situation—NYU Stern was the better business school.

For me, location was essential. NYU Stern is located in New York City, the world's business hub. New York City has countless internship opportunities, since virtually every major company is located in Manhattan. If I went to Stern, I would be able to do internships during the school year rather than just in the summer. The state business school I was accepted into was located at least five hours from New York

City, and thus I would not have access to the opportunities that NYU Stern and New York City offer. There are simply more companies and businesses in New York City than there are in a small town.

The main downside to NYU Stern is its high cost—almost twice the tuition of the state business school. This meant that all my savings from working through high school and the college savings fund and a lot of the money I'd make in the future would have to be directed to paying NYU Stern tuition.

I had a huge decision to make. I ended up choosing to attend NYU Stern, and I haven't looked back. You might think I'm crazy for picking the more expensive school, but hear me out. Everything I hoped for from NYU Stern and New York City has come to fruition. Just as my freshman year started, I was offered an internship at a major, world-renowned company. I began to think about what might have happened if I hadn't elected to go to school in New York City. What if I had gone to the state school because the tuition was lower? I wouldn't have had this internship, because I would have been attending a school five hours away from New York City. Before I even started college, my decision to head off to NYU Stern was already paying off.

And looking back now, almost three years since that internship, I can't tell you how much that opportunity jump-started my work experience—it opened the door for other internships and has since changed my life!

When it comes down to it, there is no magic formula for choosing what school to attend. There's a lot of risk involved.

For me, I rolled the dice and attended a more expensive school that I felt offered better opportunities for my career goals. There's no saying I couldn't have received a great education at the less-expensive school, but I had to go with my gut.

It's not my place to suggest where you should go to school. I mention my story to provide an alternative point of view, since many personal finance books recommend attending a school that will result in the lowest debt, without considering the student's interests or goals. You shouldn't allow the question of school costs to supersede what's best for your merits and talents. If you get accepted into a top school that's reputable in the field you want to work in, it would, in my opinion, be a mistake not to attend that school because it's expensive. While I'm certainly not an advocate of debt, it's possible to fund tuition at a top-tier school without having to touch private student loans (which you've probably heard are not friendly to students) with a ten-foot pole.

Regardless of where you go to school, it's important to know how you're going to pay the tuition, and the tools to help you are out there. So let's get down to it, shall we?

Financial Aid

The federal government provides financial aid to students in the form of loans, which need to be paid back, and grants, which do not have to be paid back (essentially free money).

To determine which of these loans and grants you will receive, you must fill out the Free Application for Federal Student Aid (FAFSA). FAFSA is undoubtedly the most important aspect of the financial aid process. FAFSA helps to determine your expected family contribution (EFC), or the amount of money the school thinks your family can afford to provide for your education. FAFSA is totally based on your family's finances, not on merit or how well you do on the SATs. The lower "net worth" your family has, generally speaking, the more aid you'll get.

The difference between the cost of college and the EFC determines how much aid you'll receive from the government. That aid can come as a combination of loans, grants, and even a work-study program (where you do work on campus, such as manning the front desk at the school gym, in exchange for $2,000 off your tuition bill). You do not get to pick which loans you receive. Colleges also use FAFSA to determine how much aid they'll give you (beyond what the federal government provides), and, of course, states also use FAFSA to determine state aid.

Aid is granted by FAFSA on a yearly basis, so if you want financial aid for all four years of college, you must reapply each year. You can fill out the FAFSA on paper or online at www.fafsa.gov. Doing it online is faster and easier, so stick with that rather than using snail mail. Deadlines vary by state and can be checked on the FAFSA website, but the form is available starting January 1 of any year. Make sure you only visit the FAFSA website maintained by the government, and not any other commercial website claiming to handle financial aid!

The FAFSA form itself is an exhaustive hundred plus-questions long. (In fact, it is so cumbersome that there are consultants out there who charge over $1,000 to fill out the form for you!) In other words, this is not something you can finish in an hour while watching *Keeping Up with the Kardashians*. Give yourself time to get it done—and us young people have heard the following cliché a million times: don't wait until the last minute!

Your parents' financial information only has to be given if you are a dependent student, as opposed to an independent student. There are numerous factors that determine whether someone is considered an independent student, including if they were born before a certain birth date (see the actual FAFSA form for the specifics); are married; are currently serving in the military; or are pursuing a graduate degree. If you're under age twenty-four, aren't married, are not serving in the military, and are not in graduate school, you're likely a dependent student.[4]

On FAFSA, you and/or your parents must enter your financial information as applicable,[5] including:

- Income
- Balance in checking/savings accounts
- Income from interest
- Value of second homes

Personal information is also needed, such as the marital status of your parents, where they went to college, Social Security numbers, addresses, and the number of people in your household. Some who apply for FAFSA will need to verify their information by providing a tax return, bank statements, or other documents. Your college will notify you if you need to do this.

It's also important to know what FAFSA does *not* consider in evaluating your financial situation. This includes:

- Retirement accounts, such as 401(k)s and IRAs
- Annuities
- Value of the home you live in
- Insurance policies

Each college you apply to will be able to see your responses on FAFSA, assuming you add the name of each college on the form. It's just like sending a report of your SAT scores to the colleges—you also have to send the college you're applying to the completed FAFSA form. Again, that's only if you want aid—and in most cases you will want aid!

A common misconception is that FAFSA is only for students and families who "don't make a lot of money." Wrong! Regardless of income level, you still have a chance of getting federal loans, and federal loans are a hell of a lot better than private loans, as you'll discover later in this chapter.

CSS Profile

If only you need to fill out just one financial aid form.

Students are very familiar with the College Board—after all, it administers the ultrafun SAT and AP tests!

Well, the College Board now offers its own financial aid form, known as the CSS Profile (College Scholarship Service

Profile). This form has the same goal as FAFSA (determining how much aid you'll receive), though its questions are much more specific and dig even deeper into your family's finances than FAFSA does. More and more colleges (especially private colleges) are requiring students to complete the CSS Profile. Be sure to check to see if the school you're applying to requires you to submit the CSS Profile. It, along with FAFSA and some school-specific forms, will determine your expected family contribution and how much aid you'll receive.

Unlike FAFSA, the CSS Profile accounts for funds in a retirement account, which will essentially make your family look wealthier, and thus could result in less aid. Additionally, home equity (the value of your parents' home, or the difference between what their home is worth and the money they owe on it through a mortgage) is accounted for in the CSS Profile.

Though some say the detailed questions help students get more aid, I'm a bit skeptical about the CSS Profile. To me, the most ridiculous part of the form is that *it costs money*. Now, if I'm in need of financial aid to pay for college, why the hell would I want to waste money on a financial aid form? The costs are a $25 set-up charge, which includes sending the report to one college (how nice of them!), and if you want to send the form to other colleges, you'll have to pay an additional $16 per college.[6] I'm shocked that colleges would jump on the bandwagon of requiring students to fill out this form, which only adds power to the already influential and wealthy College Board.

Making the financial aid process even more laborious isn't helping students who need aid. But it's certainly helping the College Board get rich.

Types of Federal Loans

Once you've completed filling out FAFSA and/or the CSS Profile, your school will send you a letter with your financial aid package, which lists how much aid you (or your parents) will receive in the form of loans, grants, and/or work-study programs.

They might offer you a package like this:

Direct PLUS Loan	$20,000
Subsidized Stafford Loan	$2,000
Pell Grant	$5,500
Work-Study Program	$2,000

Anytime you take out a loan, you will pay interest on it. So if the government gives you a $3,000 loan to help pay for college tuition, you not only have to pay back the $3,000 but the interest as well. Interest rates on government loans are rather low, in the area of 4–8 percent. Keep this in mind when reading the rest of the chapter.

Each type of federal loan is different, and some are better than others. Here is the lowdown on the different types of federal aid out there:

Direct Subsidized Loans

These are the best types of loans, because the government pays the interest on them while you're in school—and for the first six months following your graduation. That's an incredible feature that will save you tons of money.

The interest rate for direct subsidized loans for undergraduate students is 3.4 percent, and it's fixed, meaning the interest rate will not change. However, come July 1, 2013, the rate may double, to 6.8 percent, for new students who take out the loan (it won't increase for students who already have the loan). Congress decides on the interest rate. As long as you take out the loan before June 30, 2013, you will have locked in the 3.4 percent rate. Graduate students, on the other hand, always pay a 6.8 percent fixed interest rate on this type of loan.

These loans, while extremely valuable, are difficult to get. You must demonstrate a severe financial burden to qualify.

Direct Unsubsidized Loans

On the flip side, there are also direct *unsubsidized* loans. Interest on these loans starts accruing as soon as the money is applied to your tuition (that means as soon as the loan is taken out). You can start to pay the interest while in college (I highly recommended you do) or you can let the interest accrue while you're in school and start to pay it back, along with the loan amount (the principal), once you graduate. Direct unsubsidized loans have a fixed interest rate of 6.8 percent for both undergraduate and graduate students.

These loans are easier to get than direct subsidized loans—all students are eligible, regardless of their financial situation.

There are some factors that apply to *both* subsidized and unsubsidized direct loans.[7]

1. Loan Limits: There are limits as to how many of these loans you can receive. Undergraduate students can borrow between $5,500 and $12,000 each year. Students in graduate school have access to up to $20,500 a year. Again, the school determines the amount of these loans you're entitled to based on the info you provided on FAFSA and/or the CSS Profile.

2. Fees: Standard fees amounting to 1 percent are taken out of the total loan amount. So if you're offered a loan of $2,000 toward your tuition, in reality you'll only get $1,980.

3. Payment: Payment of these loans begins six months after you graduate, and if you drop out of school or "fall below half-time enrollment," well, the six-month clock starts ticking too. This six-month period is known as the grace period—it's in place to give you some time to get settled after college.

4. Promissory Note: When you receive these loans, you need to sign a promissory note, officially called a Master Promissory Note, which says you promise to pay back the loan amount, interest, and fees.

Pell Grants

If you're awarded a Pell Grant, you're a lucky guy or a gal. Pell Grants are free money—they don't have to be paid back. There is no interest either. Think of them as a gift from Uncle Sam.

The maximum Pell Grant you can receive is $5,550 for the 2012–13 school year. (The amount could slightly change depending on what Congress decides in the coming years.) The details about how the Pell Grant is awarded are pretty complex, and I don't want to bore you—all you need to know is that Pell Grants exist and, depending on your financial circumstances, you might get one, okay? Hopefully you will!

Federal Perkins Loans

Another loan option from the government is the Federal Perkins Loan. These loans are only for students with extreme financial need. Based on the info you provided on FAFSA, your school will determine if you qualify for a Federal Perkins Loan. The interest on these loans is fixed at a low 5 percent rate. Once you graduate, you have nine months until you have to start paying back the loan, as opposed to six months with the direct loans.

The maximum yearly Perkins Loan is $5,500 for undergraduates, with a total of no more than $27,500 throughout your entire college years. Graduate students can borrow a bit more, up to $8,000 per year and no more than $60,000 total.

Another perk (pun intended!) is that there are no fees associated with these loans.

PLUS Loans

What happens when you don't get enough federal aid (direct loans and Pell Grants) to cover the cost of your college tuition? Generally, the school will offer your parents a Direct PLUS Loan, which is a loan for parents who want to help fund their child's undergraduate education. Obviously, Direct PLUS Loans are only for dependent students, but if you're an independent or graduate student, don't worry, there are PLUS loans for you too!

Direct PLUS loans are very simple—the formula used to calculate the amount of these loans is:

Cost of annual tuition – financial aid = Direct PLUS Loan amount

---

So if your school costs $20,000 a year and you are awarded only $8,000 in financial aid, your parents would be offered a Direct PLUS loan for $12,000.

In order to get a Direct PLUS Loan, your parents' credit history is checked. If your parents have poor credit, they'll need to get a cosigner on the loan. This cosigner is 100 percent responsible for the loan if your parents do not pay.

Interest rates on PLUS loans are 7.9 percent, fixed, and the interest accrues right when the money is applied to the tuition. Parents must start paying back the PLUS loan within two months after the loan is taken out—there is no grace period with PLUS loans, as there is with direct subsidized and unsubsidized loans. The fees for PLUS loans are 4 percent of the loan amount.

Direct PLUS Loans are also available for independent and graduate students. The terms are the same, except that you, the student, are responsible for the loan, and it is your credit that is checked. The interest rate of 7.9 percent and 4 percent fee still apply with PLUS loans for independent and graduate students.

Hardship Letter

If there are severe financial circumstances in your family, such as job loss, salary reduction, or unbearable medical bills, then you should write a letter to the school explaining these circumstances. This is especially important if one of these financial hardships occurs after you file FAFSA.

The letter doesn't have to be a big production—one page clearly stating the situation is sufficient. It also helps to include proof of the financial hardship (such as a medical bill or a document from a former employer showing that your parent was laid off). The school may offer some sort of financial help if it deems your situation severe enough.

Paying Back Federal Loans

Now that we've discussed federal aid options, it's time to talk about paying these loans back. Putting money toward the interest while in school, even if it's just a few dollars a month, will get you out of debt faster and take some of the burden off your shoulders once you graduate.

When you graduate (or if you drop out of school or fall below half-time enrollment), you are responsible for paying back your loans. A "loan servicer"—a company like Sallie Mae, Edfinancial Services, or Direct Loans—oversees your repayment process. The loan servicer is your main point of contact for your loans, and you should call it to ask questions about the loan disbursement and to discuss your repayment options. Essentially, your student loan is passed on (and in some cases sold) to these firms. You will make the monthly payment to them rather than sending a check to the U.S. government directly. Don't panic about who your servicer will be. It'll be clear enough when the first bill comes in the mail, asking you to pay X amount of dollars. You can also check on the U.S. Department of Education's National Student Loan Data System for Students at www.nslds.ed.gov.

It goes without saying that, yes, you have to pay back your student loans. If you don't make the monthly payment on the loan, it's considered defaulting on the loan. If you default on the loan, not only will your FICO score plummet, but federal and state tax refunds can be redirected, late fees will be charged, you run the risk of getting sued, and you may not be able to get any additional federal student loans if you need them in the future. In 2009 almost 9 percent of student loans went into default.[8] So this is serious business!

There are six repayment plans for your federal student loans. Read on to find out what's best for you:

1. Standard Repayment: You are automatically enrolled into this type of repayment plan, which is the cheapest way to pay back your Federal student loans. Standard repayment means you have to make a fixed payment each month (obviously, if you can find extra money, you can always pay more than this minimum payment) for ten years.

> Since ten years is a relatively short time to pay off your student loans, your monthly payments are high, but you'll actually pay less money in interest over the life of the loan than you would with other repayment options.

> Here are some numbers to back this up. Let's say you or your parent owes $40,000 on a PLUS loan. According to the government's standard repayment calculator, your monthly payment will be about $483. By the end of the ten years, you'll actually have paid not $40,000, but $58,000, thanks to interest.

2. Extended Repayment: What if $483 a month is too much for you or your parent to afford? No worries! You can enroll in extended repayment, which, as its name suggests, stretches out your repayment period from ten years to a maximum of twenty-five years. You can only enroll in extended repayment if your loans are at least $30,000. The longer repayment results in lower monthly payments but more interest over the life of the loan.

Going back to our $40,000 PLUS loan example, under extended repayment the monthly payments would be $306, rather than the $483 under standard repayment. But with that lower $306 monthly payment, you end up paying a total of $92,000 over the twenty-five-year period, as compared to $58,000 with standard repayment. So while you do get a lower monthly payment, you're paying an extra $34,000 in interest—that's almost as much as you took out in the first place!

3. Graduated Repayment: This is a pretty innovative plan. Theoretically, as you get older and more experienced, your income should increase. So with graduated repayment, your monthly payment increases every two years—though you'll have up to ten years to pay back the loan.

Using the $40,000 PLUS loan example, monthly payments would start at $337 for the first two years of a graduated repayment plan. In the two years after that, it jumps to $408, and during the last two years (years nine and ten) the monthly payment peaks at $725. After ten years, assuming you've stuck with this plan, you'll be debt-free. Over that ten-year period, you'll pay, in addition to the $40,000 principal, some $21,500 in interest.

4. Income-Based Repayment (IBR): This is a tad tricky. Income-based repayment caps your monthly student loan payments at a percentage of your income (maximum 15 percent). The goal of IBR is to provide a monthly payment that's *less* than what it would be under standard repayment, but only if you qualify.

IBR applies to Stafford Loans, consolidation loans (more on this in a moment), and graduate PLUS loans, but *not* to parent PLUS loans or consolidation loans that include PLUS loans. Also, IBR is not for Perkins Loans, but it is for consolidation loans that include Perkins Loans. Is your head spinning yet?

Essentially, your monthly payment under IBR is based on your income and the size of your family. The monthly payment is calculated by taking 15 percent of the difference between your adjusted gross income and 150 percent of the Department of Health and Human Services Poverty Guideline.[c] The Poverty Guideline is a threshold used to determine if someone is eligible for financial assistance from the government (this could be food stamps, welfare, or federal housing projects). Your adjusted gross income is the amount of money that you have to pay taxes on (your total income less any tax deductions).

So let's do the math: Let's say you're single with a gross adjusted income of $25,000. The 2012 poverty guideline for a single person living in any state (except

Alaska and Hawaii, but including the District of Columbia) is $11,170. According to the IBR formula, we have to calculate 150 percent of that number, which is 16,755. Next, we have to take 15 percent of the difference between your adjusted gross income and the poverty guideline, which is $1,236.75. Divide this number by 12, and voilà! The monthly payment under IBR would be—$103.06.

In this specific example, you would get the green light for IBR, since the IBR payment of $103 is less than the $380 owed for standard repayment. While IBR results in a lower monthly payment than the other three repayment options we talked about, you're again stretching out the duration of the loan to twenty-five years. Don't think you're saving money with IBR—you're just kicking the can down the road. However, if you still owe a balance on your loan after twenty-five years, the remaining balance will be forgiven in some cases.

If this math scared you (flashbacks to calculus class, anyone?!), there are online calculators where you can determine whether you are eligible for IBR. Best advice, though: contact your loan servicer and ask them—they will be able to tell you if you qualify rather quickly.

5. Income-Contingent Repayment (ICR): Unlike IBR, which is based on your income and family size, income-contingent repayment also factors in the amount of debt you owe. The term of the program is twenty-five years, and any balance remaining after twenty-five years has passed will be discharged, meaning you won't be responsible for paying it. Like IBR, under ICR parent PLUS loans are excluded from the program, but all other direct loans, including PLUS loans that graduate students have, are included.

6. Income-Sensitive Repayment (ISR): This plan only applies to loans under the Federal Family Education Loan Program (FFEL). FFEL was closed down on June 30, 2010, so if you've taken out a loan after that date, this program will not apply to you. This wasn't the greatest program, anyway— it's a ten-year repayment term and your monthly payments fluctuate based on your income.

Whew! A lot to take in, right? If you're overwhelmed, it's totally understandable. To put it simply, the most financially wise option is always the standard repayment. You'll get your loans paid off in a decade and be done with it. While it does have the highest monthly payment, you'll save *thousands* of dollars in interest over the long run. But that might not always be possible, especially if you're looking for a full-time job or are working in an industry where salaries are on the low side. Only you can choose which of the repayment plans will work for you. Check out the online calculators at www.studentaid.ed.gov for each type of repayment plan. There you can enter the type of federal loan you have, its interest rate, and the balance due, and the calculator will shoot off the monthly payment.

If your financial situation changes for the better or the worse (hopefully for the better!), it is possible to switch repayment plans to fit your current financial situation. You can do so once a year—just make a call to your loan servicer and explain what plan you'd like to try.

Consolidation Loan

Aside from the financial burden of having to pay off several student loans at once, from an organizational standpoint it takes some stellar management skills to even keep track of multiple payments and stay abreast of all the due dates. To ease the stress, you can consolidate all your federal student loans into one (big) loan. No more writing three different checks for three different loans—they are all lumped together. Consolidation also allows you to extend the repayment term to thirty years, which will result in a lower payment, though more in interest costs over those thirty years. Direct subsidized and unsubsidized loans, Perkins Loans, and PLUS loans can all be consolidated. Note, however, that you cannot add *parent* PLUS loans into the mix, because those aren't loans under your name.

Consolidation essentially means that all your loans are mixed together to form a new loan with a new interest rate. That new interest rate could be higher than that of your old loans, since it is calculated by taking the weighted average of all the loans you are consolidating, and then rounding the figure up to the nearest one-eighth of a percent (though the rate cannot be more than 8.25 percent).[10] It's good to know that there's no fee attached to consolidating your loans, and you'll still have access to the different repayment plans. But even considering that, I don't see consolidation as being completely foolproof. Why run the risk of paying a higher interest rate? However, if having a new interest rate doesn't faze you and you are keen on consolidating, head over to www.loanconsolidation.ed.gov to get started.

Go Electronic

Regardless of which repayment option you chose for your federal loans, having the monthly payment automatically taken out of your checking or savings account is the best way to pay off your loans. This way you know your bill will be paid on time and in full, and you don't have to worry about mailing a check to the loan servicer or, even worse, forgetting to make your monthly payment altogether.

Contact your loan servicer and ask it to set this up for you. In fact, some loan servicers will even lower your interest rate if you sign up for automatic electronic payment!

If You're Having Trouble Paying Back Federal Loans

If you don't think you can make the payment due on your federal student loans, speak up! Don't skip paying them—the last thing you want to do is to default on your loan. Anytime you feel at risk of missing a payment, call up your loan servicer immediately. Explain that you're having trouble, and if your financial situation has been affected by dire circumstances (like a job loss or unexpected medical bill), make sure to explain that too.

You might think the servicer won't care, but it may offer you one of these options:

1. Deferment: A deferment is when your payments are "temporarily suspended." This could be for a variety of reasons, including unemployment, financial hardship, or if you're heading back to school. Interest does not accrue during deferment of direct subsidized loans and Perkins Loans; however, it does apply for direct unsubsidized loans and PLUS loans.

2. Forbearance: This is when your payments are temporarily postponed or reduced due to financial trouble. However, regardless of the type of federal loan, interest *does* accrue during forbearance, and if you don't pay the interest during this time, it will be tacked on to the principal. Forbearance is usually awarded in blocks of one year, for a maximum of three years.

Deferment and forbearance must be approved by the loan servicer. Until you've officially been told that your loans are under deferment or forbearance, you still need to make the payments—don't just assume that because you lost a job your loans are automatically on pause.

Government Loans > Private Student Loans

Sometimes federal loans won't be large enough to cover your college or graduate school tuition. The rule of thumb is to take maximum advantage of federal loans, and if they still don't cover your whole tuition, choose private student loans—and choose *wisely*.

Private student loans are disbursed by major banks like Citi, Discover, Sallie Mae, and Wells Fargo, as well as local banks and credit unions. FAFSA is *not* involved in the loan process—all you have to do is visit the bank's website and fill out the online application. The success of your loan application is largely based on your FICO score, and if you don't have one (because you don't have a credit card), or if your FICO score is low, you're going to need a cosigner. And just like a cosigner on a credit card, that person is 100 percent responsible for your loan if you can't make the payment.

The interest rates on private student loans are generally *not* fixed—they fluctuate based on market conditions. In other words, your interest rate could be 6 percent one month and jump to 6.75 percent a few months later. This is the problem with private student loans. If you're lucky enough to find a job after college, chances are you'll be living from paycheck to paycheck. And if your monthly student loan payment increases just $50 a month because your interest rate went up, well, you're likely to feel that pinch!

The only way to avoid having to worry about fluctuating interest rates is to take out a student loan with a fixed rate. During summer 2011, Wells Fargo came out with fixed-rate private student loans, and in spring 2012 private student loan giant Sallie Mae revealed a new student loan fixed at a 5.75 percent rate.[11]

At the time I'm writing this, interest rates are very low, as is generally the case when the economy is shaky. While a student loan with a variable interest rate starts off lower than a fixed-rate student loan, you run the risk of having your rate jump higher as the economy improves. No one can predict where interest rates will be in ten years, and since paying off student loans is a long-term game, it might be wise to lock in a low fixed rate right now, while interest rates are low.

Another caveat concerning private student loans: they have fees too. Some sneaky banks will advertise a student loan with a low interest rate of around 3 or 4 percent, but when you read the fine print, you'll find they charge exorbitant fees for the loan. Some are as high as an additional 5 percent, so when all is said and done, the money you save from low interest rates is almost negligible considering the high fees. Don't get tricked—always read the fine print before signing up!

Paying Back Private Loans

I wish I could say that there is a whole menu of options to choose from when it comes to paying off private student loans. But there isn't. You just have to do it. And it sucks.

Unlike federal student loans, there's no income-based repayment or graduated payment for private student loans. All the banks care about is that you write them a check. Period.

Private lenders understand that their loans are not as

sweet of a deal as the federal student loans, and as a result, they've recently started to mimic *some* of the features of federal loans. Many banks won't require you to make payments on your student loans while you're in school. The interest will still accrue during this time, but you won't have to start writing a check and making the monthly payments until you graduate or leave school. Some of the nicer private banks and lenders don't require you to start paying back your loans until six months after graduation. You may also be able to snag a lower interest rate if you enroll in automatic withdrawal or if you or your cosigner has a checking account with the bank that made the loan.[12] And if you're caught in a financial bind, certain banks are now offering deferment programs that are similar to the ones offered by the government.

Paying down interest while you're still in school is one of the best financial decisions you can make, especially if you have private loans. Even if you can only scrape up $10 or $20 a month to put toward the interest, you'll have less to pay over the life of the loan, and the number of years you'll be in debt will dramatically decrease.

Consolidation is also an available option for private loans, but I wouldn't recommend it. You can't consolidate federal student loans and private student loans, and consolidating your private student loans from multiple lenders under one main creditor won't really help you, unless your FICO score is significantly high, since the banks will determine the consolidated interest rate using your FICO score. Some banks will even charge you a fee to consolidate your loans. All in all, it's not worth it.

Graduating Early

Another way to help reduce the cost of college is to try to graduate early. Instead of attending college for four years, consider loading up on credits every semester, to graduate in three or three and a half. (And don't forget about those AP credits, if your school allows you to use them!) Of course, this isn't for everyone—it depends on your course work and your major, and it will require you to balance more classes and work. But if you're up to the challenge, it could end up saving you *thousands* of dollars.

Scholarships

Scholarships are the best type of financial aid—no interest, no fees, no nonsense.

It's easier than ever to find scholarships now, thanks to websites like Zinch.com and Fastweb.com, which list available opportunities from different organizations and interest groups. I'm talking scholarships worth $1,000 or $5,000—this isn't chump change! The best part of Zinch.com and the like is that the scholarships listed on these sites are not just for incoming college freshmen—they offer them for all undergrads.

There's no excuse not to do this—what have you got to lose? The more scholarships you are awarded, the less money you'll have to take out in loans, and I don't need to tell you why that's a good idea!

Quick Review

You just read about pretty much everything there is to know about paying for college, and it's unquestionably a complex topic. Here's what you need to remember:

1. When choosing a college, be conscious of costs, but if you get accepted into a top school that's in line with your major and career goals, weigh all the options. You could be selling yourself short if you only consider the cost.

2. Fill out the FAFSA form—this is how you'll get access to federal financial aid. You should only consider private student loans if the federal aid you receive isn't enough to cover the cost of college tuition.

3. When paying back federal loans, aim to stick with standard repayment, which has a higher monthly payment, but you'll save a ton of money in interest and get your loans paid off within ten years.

4. Just as I stressed the importance of making more than the minimum payment on credit cards, this same rule applies to student loans, whether you have federal loans or private loans or both.

9

THE ART OF THE JOB HUNT

It's no secret that our generation has gotten a bad rap. There's this notion that we're entitled, lazy, technology-addicted brats who don't understand the concept of hard work. I hate to break it to you, but this couldn't be further from the truth. I see my peers out there hustling every day—whether it's managing a double major, working three jobs, or even starting their own businesses. We are a generation of achievers. (They might be right about the technology-addicted part though. So sue us!)

A shaky economy and job market is scary for anyone but especially for young people. We have to fight for entry-level jobs and internships in a sea of hungry applicants. There was one summer when I applied for every part-time job in my neighborhood—from retail stores to Whole Foods—and didn't get *one* response. This may have happened to you too, and if it has, I know you'll agree—it sucks, plain and simple. But these challenges also make us stronger, whether you realize it or not. We work harder to prove ourselves. We know

that we can't settle for being average. We aren't a lazy generation. We're a motivated one, ready to tackle what's ahead.

It's easy to get discouraged or nervous about landing a job
when stakes are so high, but I want to tell you that you're not
alone. You never know where life is going to lead you. Maybe
you'll strike gold and land your dream job right out of school.
Maybe you'll have to work a string of unpaid internships before finding a career path you love. Maybe you'll be forced to
take a job you're not thrilled with out of financial obligation.
Regardless of the circumstances, you'll be able to get where
you want to go eventually. Don't give up on yourself! Believe
in your capabilities, and picture yourself in your dream job. If
you can imagine it, you can take the steps to achieve it. Being
negative isn't productive. When your friends, teachers, professors, spiritual adviser, significant other, or even parents tell
you the job market is tough and you'll never find a job, tune
them out!

You only need *one* job to get you on the right path. And
that's what this chapter is about—landing that job or that internship is the first step in your journey to doing what you
love. From how to ace that interview to résumé writing to
using Twitter and LinkedIn to find internships—I've got you
covered!

What Do You Want to Do?

Life is a bit easier if you're excited about what you want to do.
Some people know early on that they want to be doctors, law-

yers, or businesspeople. Others take a few years to experiment and see what they like and what they don't like. As long as you can find something you are passionate about, you're setting yourself up to succeed. And I know this is a cliché—but I guarantee you it's the case—anytime a megasuccessful person is interviewed on television, you hear them say, "Love what you do." It makes sense. If you find a career that you truly enjoy, then it's not work. And because you like it, you'll be better at it.

Regardless of where you are in life—about to enter college, in college, or stuck at a dead-end job after college—thinking hard about what you like and what you want to do is an incredibly important first step.

In middle school and high school, I always thought a career in business was for me. But as I started taking classes in college, I realized my true passion was to get involved in business journalism and broadcasting. While it's not totally unrelated to a job in finance, realizing that's where my interest lay was still a pivotal moment for me.

Internships are a great way to get your feet wet and to help narrow the scope of what you like and don't like in a potential job. Think about it: for two or three months, you get to be a fly on the wall at a real company or organization, experiencing its day-to-day office culture. I've had six internships so far, and they have been great opportunities to narrow down what I want in my future career. You can do this too! Read on to find out how you can land one.

Get That Résumé Ready

Before we talk about how to find internships, we need to polish up your résumé. You probably already have one, but I want to share some dos and don'ts when it comes to résumés.

Here's how my résumé is formatted:

Scott Gamm

Address	Phone Number	E-mail Address

EDUCATION_____

New York University—Leonard N. Stern School of Business—2014
- *Major:* Finance/Marketing

EXPERIENCE_____

Name of Company
Title   *Starting Month/Year–Ending Month/Year*
- Brief description of what I did at the job
- Brief description of what I did at the job

Name of Company
Title   *Starting Month/Year–Ending Month/Year*
- Brief description of what I did at the job
- Brief description of what I did at the job

Name of Company
Title   *Starting Month/Year–Ending Month/Year*
- Brief description of what I did at the job
- Brief description of what I did at the job

TECHNICAL SKILLS & INTERESTS_____

- *Skills:* Excel, iNews, iMovie, Photoshop, WordPress
- *Interests:* Cycling, golf, drumming, and travel

Notice how I have my full name in bold at the top? This sounds like a no-brainer, but it's imperative that you keep your contact information at the top of the page. You want to make it as easy as possible for the employer to contact you. Name, address, telephone number, and e-mail address should be displayed prominently. And, please, keep your e-mail address professional. There's no way I'm going to land a job with an e-mail address like ScottyG@gmail.com. Whatever you do, don't put an embarrassing or immature sounding e-mail address on your résumé.

For those of us in school or just out, it's important to start the résumé with your education—the name of the school you attended, along with your major and minor. You should list relevant activities (editor of the school newspaper, etc.) and your GPA if it is above 3.0. Any academic awards, including whether you were inducted into an honor society or made the dean's list, should be included in this section of the résumé.

When listing jobs or internships on your résumé, start with the current or most recent one and work backward chronologically. Notice how I start with the company's name, and then I put my title, "intern," below it. You want the company name to stand out—everyone knows that at this young age you didn't have a fancy title.

Next, I added two (three is fine too) brief bullet points explaining my responsibilities at the job. Now, here's where this gets a bit tricky. You want to impress employers, but not to the point where they think you're embellishing your responsibilities. Here's an example: Let's say you interned at an asset management firm, which is an organization that manages and invests the money of various clients.

Your role at the firm *probably* was along these lines:

- Assist managers with researching stocks, bonds, and investments

But if you write the following on your résumé, don't expect anyone to trust you:

- Met with and advised clients to ensure proper asset allocation and facilitated the company's proprietary stock trades

Nobody is going to believe a twenty-year-old intern actually met with the firm's clients and told them what investments they should buy. Now, this is an extreme example, but the point is don't exaggerate your responsibilities and roles at past jobs or internships. Include realistic descriptions of what you did, and make them dynamic and specific. Active verbs like "assisted," "prepared," "wrote," and "designed" sound proactive and professional. (Unless you are currently working at the internship, these verbs should be in the past tense, not the present.) When you can, use numerical quantities: "Assisted in the preparation of ten briefs for two head managers," or "Wrote copy for five potential ads."

If you've never interned before, don't sweat it. You should include any part-time jobs you've held and any volunteer work you've done in the past. That stuff is totally valid and admirable!

You never want your résumé to be longer than a single

page, but you don't want it to have a ton of blank space either. If you still have room after listing your internships and work experience, include some basic technical skills and interests. I wouldn't list that you know how to use Microsoft Office, since that's pretty standard these days, but if you know how to use programs like Excel or Photoshop, that's worth mentioning.

Now let's talk about some résumé don'ts:

1. Awards on your résumé should be from your college years—try to limit the high school stuff as much as possible. Sorry to burst your bubble, but no one's really going to care that you were in the math league or on the swim team when you were fifteen.

2. Some people have an "objectives" section of their résumé, which is usually at the top, right below the name and contact information. This is where you write what you're hoping to gain out of a future job and what makes you stand apart from other job applicants. I would *not* include an "objectives" section. It's a waste of time and space, and they sound generic and redundant. You'll be able to express yourself much more clearly in your cover letter.

3. Keep the fonts neutral (no fancy script or cute lettering) and only print in black and white.

4. Don't just write one draft of the résumé and call it a day. Ask friends and family or even the career services department at your school to edit it. It's not something you can slap together during the commercial breaks while watching *Jersey Shore*.

Finding the Job

Okay, so now that we've got your résumé, it's time to find the job or internship of your dreams! Whether you're in school and looking for an internship or out of school looking for a full-time job, the same principles apply.

It seems like a daunting task, but I'm here to tell you it *can* be done! There are more tools out there than ever to help you find a job. Here are some of the best methods:

1. Career Fairs: If you're in college or grad school, chances are your school will offer a career fair where employers will set up a table and briefly talk to students—sometimes one-on-one and sometimes in a small group. When attending a career fair, you should be dressed professionally and have your résumé in hand in case the employer asks for it. Career fairs seem intimidating, since you have a bunch of students walking around trying to make a good impression and essentially competing for the same few jobs. Ignore your nerves. Just walk up to the employers' representatives confidently, listen to their descriptions, and ask them a few questions about the jobs. You should also be ready to give a thirty-second pitch about you and your interests if the position sounds enticing.

2. Social Media: Some three hundred to five hundred jobs are posted on Twitter every minute, according to

Tweetajob.com.[1] Sites like that and TwitJobSearch.com are excellent ways to find job postings. On these sites, you can type in the name of a company (like accounting firm Ernst & Young) or the name of an industry (like "graphic design" or "technology") and find a list of related jobs.

> After you type in your company or industry of choice, the site will show you all the tweets that relate to your search area. Next you can click on the View Job button next to each tweet, and the site will direct you to the original job listing. It's that easy!

3. Your School's Database: Some schools offer their own database of job openings and internships. If yours doesn't, it probably has a career services office. See if someone there can help you find jobs or at least edit your résumé and cover letters.

4. Company Presentations: At my school, many of the major banks will give presentations to students. Unlike a career fair, where dozens of companies set up booths in one room, these events are specifically for one company. Students listen to presentations from recruiters, senior managers, and even alumni who now work there. This is a great opportunity to meet people and learn about what a typical day at the company is like.

> Try to get the business cards of the people you meet—you can even go as far as sending them a thank-you e-mail the following day.

Show Your Interest

At these company presentations, you usually have to sign in or fill out a card with your name and basic contact info. If you end up applying for a job there later on, the application might ask if you have attended one of these events. If you did, make sure you note it. Attending these events might score you some extra brownie points, since it shows you took the time to learn more about the company.

5. Applying Online: Hey, sometimes it just takes visiting the company's or organization's website and seeing if there are any openings. All you have to do is scroll down to the bottom of the page where it says Careers or About Us. If you don't see job listings on those pages, do some digging on the site, or simply Google "jobs at Company X" or "internships at Company X."

Some people don't like this option, since they feel they're sending their résumé into space and no one will ever see it. But this is how I found the internship I had last summer. A month after I applied on the company's website, I received an e-mail asking me to come into the office for an interview. To me, that reaffirmed the value of applying online.

6. Plain Old Word of Mouth: There's no shame in asking around about open positions. Professors, former bosses, and even Facebook friends could have leads to interesting jobs. You'll never know unless you put yourself out there!

Cover Letters

All right, so now you've got a sharp résumé and a job you're dying to get. The next step is to write a brilliant cover letter. A cover letter helps the employer to get a sense of who you are and why you would be a good person to hire for the position. It's the first thing an employer looks at, so it's gotta be perfect!

Cover letters are written in paragraph form—save the bullets for your résumé. They shouldn't be a summary of your résumé; instead think of a cover letter as a coherent, well-written story.

There is no magic formula for writing a solid cover letter. Just like you would write any formal letter, start by listing your name, address, phone number, and e-mail address. You should direct the letter to whoever is reviewing your résumé. Sometimes the address given is a general e-mail address (careers@companyX.com or info@companyX.com) or sometimes it's the e-mail address of a person (like John .Smith@companyX.com or Jsmith@companyX.com). Obviously, if given a name, address the e-mail or cover letter to that person. But if there is no name given, address it to "Dear Sir or Madam," "Dear Human Resources Department," or the old, reliable "To Whom It May Concern." You should also include the physical address of the company below your address, even if you don't know the specific name of the hiring manager.

Sending a Blank E-Mail

Unless the company gives specific instructions to do so, do not, under any circumstances send a blank e-mail with your cover letter and résumé attached. Instead copy and paste your cover letter into the body of the e-mail and attach your résumé to the e-mail as a PDF or Word document. A blank e-mail will surely get deleted or viewed as a virus or spam!

It's pretty common to start your cover letter with "My name is _____ and I am a junior at X College." News flash—no one cares what your name is! They may in twenty years, but not right now. Ditch that generic and amateurish opener for something with a little more pizzazz.

A cleaner opening to your cover letter would be, "As a junior _____ major at X College, I have previously interned at _____ and am passionate about the _____ industry because _____." If you're a recent grad, you could say, "As a 2013 graduate of _____ . . ."

At the very beginning of your cover letter, it's also important to make clear what position you are applying for. Something as simple as "I am currently seeking the _____ position at Company X" is sufficient.

Your second and third paragraphs should detail why you are *the* candidate this company should hire. These paragraphs shouldn't be a laundry list of your past work experiences—that's what your résumé is for, after all. Before you launch into reasons why you are an ideal candidate, carefully read the job or internship description. In that description, the employer will list the duties of the job. You want to reference these in the cover letter. Now, don't specifically say, "according to the job description." Subtly add these references into the mix. If the job description says strong public speaking skills are required, and you have specific experience in public speaking from an internship or volunteer activity, the cover letter is a great place to discuss this qualification. You could be a totally qualified candidate for a certain position, but if you don't properly present the skills the employer wants to see in a candidate, you could be overlooked. So sell yourself and your appropriate skills as best you can!

Don't be pushy or overzealous in the letter. Lines like "I am confident I will hear from you soon" or "Please let me know ASAP if I got the job" are unprofessional. Instead end the cover letter by thanking the employer for its consideration and mention that you have enclosed your résumé for review. Include your contact information at the end of the cover letter too.

Since you'll probably be applying for multiple jobs and internships, it's crucial to make each cover letter specific to the company. Using the same cover letter for all the jobs you're applying for is dangerous. Employers will notice when you use a standard cover letter, and to them it demonstrates a lack of interest.

Once you've clicked on Submit Application or sent the

e-mail to that general address, wait about two to three weeks. If you don't hear anything, it's time to check in and send a follow-up e-mail. This is more effective if the company provided a name or e-mail address of someone at the firm— sending it to a general-inquiries e-mail is probably not going to help you. So if you do have the person's name, send an e-mail like this:

> Dear Mr. Jones,
>
> I recently applied for the summer internship program at Company X. I wanted to reach out to see if there is any more information I can provide, in addition to my résumé, which I submitted on [insert the date you applied for the job].
>
> As a student [or recent graduate] of/at [name of school], I am passionate about the [name of industry— maybe it's media, public relations, corporate finance] and look forward to the possibility of joining the Company X team this summer.
>
> Thank you for your consideration.
>
> > Best,
> >
> > [Your name]
> >
> > [Your contact information]

See how the e-mail is short and to the point? You're rolling the dice, but this strategy is certainly better than sitting back and waiting for the phone to ring! If nothing else, it'll show the company that you're proactive.

Get on LinkedIn, Now!

You're probably already on Facebook, maybe even Twitter, but what about LinkedIn? LinkedIn is another social networking site, but it's for the workplace. It may not be as fun as some of those other sites, but being on LinkedIn will be infinitely more helpful to you than playing FarmVille could ever be.

Think of LinkedIn as an electronic résumé that anyone can access. You create a profile that represents your professional experiences, including:

1. Your current title/position
2. Your past internships or jobs
3. The name of the school(s) you attend or attended (along with your major)
4. A picture of yourself (make sure it's a professional picture, not one of you holding a beer!)
5. Links to your Twitter handle (only post yours if it is work-appropriate!)
6. You can even ask past bosses or coworkers to write a brief letter of recommendation to be posted on your LinkedIn page, so people can see how great you are!

Instead of "friending" people as you would on Facebook or "following" people as you would on Twitter, on LinkedIn you "connect" with people. Just like you can search any name on Facebook and pull up that person's Facebook page, you can do the same on LinkedIn, to find, for example, their title and where they work.

Some people say that LinkedIn is helpful in finding a job. It's not a job search engine per se, though it does have areas where it recommends jobs that are open in your field.

Honestly, LinkedIn is more a point of protocol these days. You have to assume that an employer will Google your name, and if you have a LinkedIn page, it will come up in the results. If you don't have a LinkedIn page, it shows employers that you're not tech savvy. So get on it already, will ya?

Acing Interviews

Oh, the dreaded interview. So much pressure! From how you come across during the interview, to what you're wearing—it seems as if there are fifty cameras pointed at you, watching and analyzing every hand gesture and word you say. And then, of course, during the interview, and before and after, the possibility of you *not* getting the job crosses your mind. Let's forget about that thought for one moment. Yes, your performance needs to be impeccable, but that is totally doable.

In most cases, a potential candidate has to go through a series of interviews. Think of it as a video game—each interview is a different level, and you have to be really good to make it to the next stage. Usually the interviews are in person (you would either go to the company's offices or perhaps meet at a nearby coffee shop), but sometimes they are conducted by phone or even on Skype. You'll typically start out with an interview by someone in the HR department (a.k.a. "the recruiter") and if they like you, they'll set up another interview with someone in the department where you would potentially work. Finally, your potential boss will interview you. Each organization and firm has its own system of interviews, but this sequence is fairly standard.

The goal of an interview is essentially to see how well you get along with your potential boss. Think about it: if you're going to be working for them, they have to like you and know that you're going to do a good job without requiring much supervision. So be your best self—likable, personable, and confident. You can do it!

Here Are My Top-Five Tips for Nailing an Interview:

1. Dress Well: This is so important. Dressing casually for an interview is a *big* no-no. I understand that lots of industries care less and less about workplace attire these days, but for an interview, it's critical to dress well. Use your judgment—you know what's appropriate and not appropriate. No flip-flops, no jeans, no miniskirts. Aim to dress more conservative, rather than less, even in a creative industry. And whatever you do, don't ask the interviewer what you should wear—that's just an amateur move.

2. Body Language: A strong handshake and good posture make a great impression. Harvard Business School professor Amy Cuddy says good posture is key. In a May 2012 *Wired* article, she says, "You don't want to go in and be totally dominant. But do make yourself as big as you can in a way that feels natural. The power posing beforehand is the way to optimize your brain. It's not that it makes you smarter or more likable. It affects your speaker presence—your confidence, enthusiasm, and ability to captivate."[2]

3. Speak Up! If your voice cracks or gets significantly lower in volume at the end of each sentence, it's a sign of weakness. You don't need to scream, but conveying a sense of confidence and alertness is critical. Speaking softly or failing to enunciate your words isn't going to make a good impression, especially if it's a job where you'll be working the phones or dealing with the public.

> How do you correct this issue of sounding like a mouse? Practice! Look into the mirror or, better yet, record yourself speaking. Or have a parent or friend do interview run-throughs with you to practice your answers. Watch cable news channels to see examples of anchors and reporters who speak (and argue!) very well, and follow their lead.

4. Become an Expert: This also could be called *research the hell out of this position*. When you walk into that interview, you want know everything about that company or organization. Know who the CEO is, when it was founded, and if the company has been in the news lately. Take an hour or two the day before the interview and research, research, research! This doesn't mean you should start spouting off random facts about the company during the interview to show off. But I guarantee you'll be asked why you want to work at this specific company, and it'll help if you come across as knowledgeable and as passionate as possible about the place you're hoping to work.

A great way to find recent news about a company is to view their latest press releases, which are almost always posted on their website. Or type the name of the company into Google News to find the latest articles written about it.

5. No Rambling: When responding to the interviewer's questions, there's a science to how you fire back. Think of your responses as a story with a beginning, middle, and end. As soon as you feel you're rambling on, or see the interviewer lean back in their chair (which is a sign that they're losing interest in what you're saying), wrap up your response quickly. If you're prone to rambling when you're nervous, take a deep breath and pause before you launch into a response.

6. Ask Questions: At the end of almost every interview, the recruiter will ask if you have any questions. If you politely shake your head no, you're making a mistake. Always be prepared with at least one question. The interviewers love this. "What is a typical day like here?" "Where do you see the future of the industry going?" or "What do you like best about your job?" are all pointed, professional questions.

With these tips in hand, you're sure to make a great impression!

Don't Forget Your Manners

Sending a thank-you within twenty-four hours of an interview is very important. Don't expect a response—it's more about protocol and giving a professional impression.

Here's a thank-you e-mail I recently sent to an interviewer a few hours after we met—and I got the job:

> Hi _____,
>
> It was great to see you today. It sounds like you've designed an in-depth and well-rounded internship program, and I am excited about the opportunity to join the [company name] this summer.
>
> As mentioned, I view business news as the core of what people want to hear about, and I would be thrilled to expand my experience in network news to cover stories that affect the city I love.
>
> Thanks very much, and I look forward to speaking soon.
>
> Best,
>
> Scott
>
> Scott Gamm
> Phone:
> E-mail:

By the way, if a day has passed and you haven't sent the thank-you e-mail, don't bother sending it—you'll just look disorganized and forgetful.

Sending a handwritten thank-you note is also a way to stand out from the competition. Just make sure the card is professional and that your message is neat and succinct. Send this card out on the day of your interview, so the interviewer receives it sooner rather than later.

Your Action Plan

We just spoke about the many moving parts in the job/internship hunting process—from polishing your résumé and cover letter to finding the position to acing the interview. To put this all together, I've drawn up a step-by-step action plan.

Let's say your goal is to have a summer internship at a bank. Here's a sample schedule to follow, which you'll want to start at least three months before the internship deadline:

Three Months Before the Internship Deadline:

- Week 1: Polish your résumé and cover letter.
- Week 2: Meet with a career counselor at your school's career center; if you're an alum, go back to the school.
- Week 3: Search online for ten internship positions at local banks, national banks, and investment banks and apply for them!
- Week 4: Wait and be proud of the work you've already accomplished.

Two Months Before the Internship Deadline:

- Week 1: Be on the lookout for any career and internship fairs on your campus or at your alma mater.
- Weeks 2–3: If you haven't heard back from any of the positions, check the status of your application.
- Week 4: Search for another five to eight internships in a related field, to act as a plan B in case you don't hear back from the original ten companies.

Paid versus Unpaid Internships

Obviously, paid internships are preferable—working for free is never easy. I've worked as an unpaid intern for a total of four semesters. Sure it would have been nice to be paid, but the opportunity and value of being at the companies was priceless. In my case, working unpaid internships was a stepping-stone to finding two paid internships later on.

And don't get the impression that paid internships are nonexistent. The National Association of Colleges and Employers asked 280 organizations, and collectively they expect to hire forty thousand interns in 2012—up 8.5 percent from 2011.[3] And almost all the companies said they're hiring *paid* interns. Cool, right?

So don't be an intern snob—working as an unpaid intern is better than doing the following:

- Stalking friends on Facebook
- Watching *Teen Mom*
- Trying to scout out bars that don't card

And if you can snag one of those coveted paid internships, all power to you!

Making Your Internship Work

You're wasting your time interning if you just sit in the office all day and do nothing. At times there may not be enough work to do, so be proactive. Always ask your supervisor if there's anything you can do. If they don't think of anything, create a job for yourself. Don't use this time to go on Google Chat or upload pictures to Facebook.

My internships were in the media industry. When there wasn't enough to do, I would pitch story ideas to editors. It turned out great—I got more writing experience and kept busy, and it made my bosses' job a bit easier. Your internship experience is ultimately summed up by how much you put into it—the more, the better!

Don't come into your internship expecting to run the place. You're there to learn, and to do that you have to start at the bottom. Some of your tasks might not be the most glamorous, but do them with gusto anyway. You've all heard the stories about interns who have to fetch the coffee—if that's your task, then make sure it's the best damn cup of coffee in the world. I've never had to get coffee for bosses during my internships, but I did occasionally make photocopies. And, you know what? I don't have any complaints. We all have to start somewhere, so be humble. These tasks aren't beneath you! Nobody likes an intern with a bad attitude, so put your best foot forward and make yourself helpful in every task, big or small.

Getting to know your boss and the rest of the staff at the internship is key. Ask to go to lunch with your boss or at least a meeting over coffee so you can learn about his or her career path. And when your internship is over, please, please, please remember to send a handwritten thank-you card. Your supervisors and coworkers will be great resources to help you find a full-time job when you need it, so leave the best impression possible!

Quick Review

What good is having money-management skills if you have no money? Here's what you want to take away from this chapter on jobs and internships so you can be on your way to making the big money someday:

1. Figuring out where your passions lie is the best way to decide what industry you want to work in. And remember, career decisions aren't permanent!

2. The first step to landing that job is a perfect résumé and a cover letter that makes recruiters excited about having you join their company. Research the position, and never send out a generic cover letter.

3. When searching for jobs, don't rely on one strategy. Attend career fairs, apply online, use social media— heck, you may even post a status update on Facebook to see if your friends know of any internship openings. Don't stop!

4. Acing your interviews ultimately comes down to how

well you speak and the content of your responses. Be polished and practice.

5. And once you're on the job, get busy! Whether it's creating jobs for yourself or running errands, be indispensable to your boss.

10

WHAT RETIREMENT?

We've discussed a lot of issues that are probably affecting you right now: creating a budget, climbing out of credit card debt, figuring out the best student loans. But now I'm going to ask you to consider something that won't affect you today or tomorrow or even ten years from now: your retirement. I know, I know. You're probably thinking, "Are you kidding, Scott? Retiring is the furthest thing from my mind right now. I'm worried about *getting* a job!" But hear me out. Planning for your retirement now is one of the best financial moves you could *ever* make in your life.

Unless you're Betty White, you're going to be too old to work someday. Most people retire in their midsixties, but lately, with the economic troubles, people are delaying their retirement to give them some extra time to bolster their savings. You don't want to be that person. Would you rather be the hip old guy or lady in Palm Beach, sipping martinis and playing golf when you're seventy, or someone who is still slaving away in an office? I know which option I'd prefer. So the time to start saving is now.

Saving for retirement when you're young is great because you have an incredibly long period of time to get your money to grow. Remember when we talked about compounding interest in chapter 2? The same principle applies to retirement savings. Compounding interest works much more effectively when you have more time on your side, so the earlier you start saving for retirement, the better. Your goal is to put 10–15 percent of your income toward retirement each year. That may sound like a ton of money, but I promise it'll be worth it!

Most people fund their retirement through a combination of Social Security money, pension allotment, and savings in retirement accounts like 401(k)s and Roth IRAs. Let's talk about each of these options, and then lay out the best plan so you can retire with style.

Social Security

Social Security is a monthly check provided by the government. If you take a look at your pay stub, you'll see FICA (Federal Insurance Contributions Act), or Social Security tax, deducted from your paycheck. It's pretty sad to see that money go, but it's for a reason. The money taken out of your paycheck goes to pay for those who are retired right now, and when you reach retirement age, those younger than you who are still working will finance your Social Security check. You're supposed to get this money when you retire (you need to be at least sixty-two years of age).

You may have heard that there's a Social Security crisis in this country and that there won't be enough money left in Social Security to finance our generation's retirement. This isn't a fear-mongering political tactic; it's a legitimate concern. Social Security is not sustainable in its current model. With the retirement age set at sixty-two and life expectancies rising, the government has to pay more and more money each year to fund senior citizens. In our lifetime, you should expect to see Social Security taxes go up and the money you receive from the program when you retire go down. This is why it's important to take matters into your own hands by saving for retirement on your own—Social Security isn't secure.

Pension

These days pensions are generally connected to civil service or government jobs, like being a teacher, police officer, firefighter, or mail carrier. Private companies rarely offer pensions anymore.

Here's how a pension works. Let's say your mother is a teacher, and after thirty years, her annual salary is $60,000 a year. Once she retires, she would get a pension, which would be a percentage of that $60,000 salary paid to her for the rest of their life. Not a bad deal.

Even if you plan to work in a government job for the rest of your life, there's no guarantee that you'll get a pension. Pensions are on their way out as both the government and companies are tightening their purse strings. Notice a pattern?

401(k)

Here's where we start talking about what *you* can do to get a head start on your retirement savings: alas, we stumble upon the 401(k).

401(k) plans are offered by companies so that their employees can invest for retirement safely and securely. An employee elects how much money they'd like to set aside toward their 401(k), and the money is taken directly from their paycheck and placed into an account, tax-free. While the contribution limits are always subject to change, in 2013, you could contribute a maximum of $17,500 a year to your 401(k). Quick challenge: forgo one beer a week for a year and throw that money into your 401(k), okay? Note, these contribution limits are subject to change each year. As an added bonus, your employer may choose to match the amount you put in or at least kick in a percentage—perhaps 50 percent of every dollar you put in. Some employers don't contribute anything, though. If you're working at a tech start-up, don't expect much of a contribution from your employer. But if you're working at a Microsoft-type company, that's where you can benefit from a substantial contribution. Once your money goes into the 401(k), you should act like it doesn't exist. You're allowed to withdraw the money from the account any time *after* age 59.5, and when you do, you'll have to pay ordinary income taxes on it.

Talk to your human resources department about setting up a 401(k). The folks there will have all the info you need about how much you want to contribute and how much (if any) your employer contributes. If your employer matches what you contribute, then it's best contribute up to the maximum level, since, well, the employer's share is essentially free money.

Your 401(k) isn't just an account to hold your money, like a savings account. You're actually investing money into various vehicles, whether stocks, bonds, or mutual funds. The way the money is invested in your 401(k) is known as your "asset allocation."

Common Investments You Should Know

When tackling retirement accounts, it helps to have a basic understanding of stocks, bonds, and mutual funds—so let's elaborate:

1. Stocks: Come on, you've heard of stocks before. Any major company (like Apple, Microsoft, Facebook, or Exxon Mobil) and some smaller companies are publicly traded on either the New York Stock Exchange or the NASDAQ. And this means you, the investor, can buy a piece (a very small piece) of these companies. The goal is to buy the stock when the price falls and later sell it at a higher price for a profit. It's easier said than done—if we could all nail this very delicate sequence, well, let's just say that none of us would show up for work tomorrow!

2. Bonds: Bonds are a bit more complex. But let's say a company needs to raise money to develop a new product, or maybe a local government needs money to build a new park, or the federal government needs money. Companies will issue corporate bonds, local and state governments will issue municipal bonds, and the federal government will issue Treasuries.

You can "invest" in the bond, and it will grow and mature with an interest rate "attached" to it known as the "coupon."

3. Mutual Funds: Mutual funds are a combination of different investment vehicles. A mutual fund manager picks and chooses various stocks, bonds, and other investments and meshes them together into a fund. Some of these funds have fees that go to the manager, others don't. The ones that don't are called "no-load" mutual funds, and they are the best ones to invest in.

You may have heard that investing in stocks is a lot like playing roulette at the Mandalay Bay in Vegas, and it is. But since you're young, you have the time to take on that extra risk. And we all know that with more risk comes more reward.

Here's a quick checklist for keeping your 401(k) spic-and-span, especially when you start a new job and are thrown a bunch of papers about it:

1. Choosing Investments: Your employer likely uses a firm to manage its employees' 401(k) accounts. Look for investments with the lowest fees. The term "expense ratio" is another word for a fee attached to an investment, so look for investments with a low expense ratio, ideally under 1 percent.

2. 401(k) Fees: Be mindful of the fees you're paying for your 401(k). A report from Demos showed that a couple could pay more than $155,000 in 401(k) fees over their lifetime.[1] Beginning July 1, 2012, the companies that manage your

401(k) (like Fidelity, for example) will have to disclose to your employer the fee breakdown for your 401(k), and your employer is mandated to pass this info along to you.[2] You can then determine if it's too costly to maintain the 401(k). If that is the case, it might be best to opt for a different type of retirement savings plan. We'll discuss those soon.

3. Target Date Funds: If you don't want to choose from the investment options your employer offers in its 401(k), you'll be enrolled in what's known as a "target date fund," or the standard 401(k) investment. Target date funds are good, especially if you are young. Remember how we've talked about the importance of taking on a bit more risk in your investments when you're young? Well, target date funds do just that. If you're in your early twenties, your target date fund will be invested primarily in stocks, which are much riskier than bonds or mutual funds. As you get older, the fund will pivot and invest in fewer stocks, instead favoring safer investments like bonds. Why? Because you're getting closer to retirement, which means you're going to need this money soon, and it doesn't make sense fooling around with risky stocks when you're fifty-five years old! You don't want to lose your money in the eleventh hour.

Early Withdrawal

If you withdraw money from your 401(k) before age 59.5, you'll have to pay ordinary income tax on the money at that time, along with a 10 percent penalty for early withdrawal. So if you withdraw $10,000 from your 401(k) at age thirty-five to pay off credit card debt, not only will you have to pay income taxes on that amount, but you'll have to pay the 10 percent penalty, in this case $1,000.

When an emergency hits—like job loss or an unexpected health emergency—you may need to dip into your 401(k) as a last resort. But to use it to finance home renovations or weddings, as some people do, well, that's just plain stupid! Again: pretend as if the money in your 401(k) doesn't exist until you retire. You don't want to touch it.

Roth IRA

Here's a crazy statistic to consider: if you save $1,000 a year—that's $83.33 a month—from now until age sixty-five, you could end up with more than $250,000 in your bank account when you retire.

And that's assuming an annual return of 7 percent, which is a bit modest.

Now . . . let's say you decided to spend that $1,000 each year at Starbucks throughout your twenties. Come age thirty you finally get some sense and ditch the Fraps and put that money into savings. Now how much would you have at age sixty-five? Well, again, assuming a 7 percent annual return, you would have $148,000.

So eight years of buying Starbucks made you lose $117,000!

When I say "save $83.33 per month," I don't mean stuffing it into a piggy bank or even a regular savings account.

Enter the best weapon in your arsenal of savings tactics: the Roth IRA. A Roth IRA (Individual Retirement Account) is arguably the most important financial tool you could have. It's a retirement account that is independent of an employer, so if your employer doesn't offer a 401(k), doesn't match any contributions, or the fees are exorbitant, the Roth IRA is the answer. In fact, even if your employer does offer a great 401(k), you *still* want to have a Roth IRA. The more retirement savings you have, well, the better your life will be when you're older!

A Roth IRA works differently than a 401(k). With a Roth IRA, you are depositing money that you've *already* paid taxes on. The money isn't deducted from your paycheck; you put funds in the account by your own volition, with a maximum contribution for 2013 of $5,500 a year. The same rules apply, in that you can't withdraw money from a Roth IRA before age 59.5 without facing a penalty. But when you do reach that age and want to withdraw the money, you don't pay any taxes on that amount or the profit you've made from investing that money; you already paid tax on the original amount when you deposited it.

You can also withdraw your original contributions at any time without a penalty, even before age 59.5, just not the gains you've made on the contributions. So if you deposited $2,000 into a Roth IRA and that $2,000 grew to $2,300, you can withdraw that $2,000 at any time, but not the $300, since that amount is considered gains. But let's not get into the habit of withdrawing *any* money from your Roth IRA, okay? It's not a savings account—it's money to be used forty years from now.

Opening up a Roth IRA is similar to opening up a checking or a savings account. Instead of heading to Chase or Bank of America, you'll head to a discount brokerage firm, like Scottrade, Fidelity, Vanguard, or T. Rowe Price. And you can easily open the account online if you don't want to go in person. They'll ask for standard information, but be aware of one piece of information that may not occur to you naturally: the Social Security number of your beneficiary (the person who will take over your account if you die, like a parent, sibling, or relative).

When opening your Roth IRA, you may have to immediately deposit $1,000 as a minimum balance. You shouldn't have to pay a fee to open the account (so if you're charged a fee, you're being ripped off). I highly recommend opting for automatic withdrawal into your account—it'll make it harder for you to skip on payments.

Usually your income increases as you age, whether from more experience, promotions, or even inheritances (hey, you never know!). To contribute to a Roth IRA as a single person in 2013, you have to earn less than $112,000 a year. So open up that Roth IRA as soon as possible, before your income increases. And when I say now, I mean now.

If your employer has a robust 401(k) program (low fees, it matches part of your contributions), then you should contribute to the 401(k) to take advantage of the "free money" your employer kicks in. But if you can swing it, open up a Roth IRA to watch your money grow tax-free. Remember, your goal is to save 10–15 percent of your annual income for retirement purposes.

Roth 401(k)

Okay, so what if we could pick and choose the benefits of the 401(k) and the Roth IRA and mesh them into one "dream" account? Yes, such a thing exists and it's aptly called a Roth 401(k)—very creative, I know!

Roth 401(k)s combine the best elements of a Roth IRA and a 401(k). The money you contribute to a Roth 401(k) is money you've already paid taxes on, so you don't have to pay taxes when you withdraw the money after you reach age 59.5. Another great benefit is that your employer can contribute and match some of your contributions. And remember how we said that if you make over a certain amount of money, you won't qualify for a stand-alone Roth IRA? Well, there are no income restrictions with a Roth 401(k) and you can even contribute more to a Roth 401(k) than you can to a Roth IRA—a maximum of $17,000 per year.

Roth 401(k)s are offered only through employers, and they aren't always available. Talk to your HR department to see if your employer offers it and if they do, you better jump at the opportunity.

Quick Review

This chapter was full of technical terms and rules, which might have given you a headache. But, hey, investing well can result in some big bucks when we get older, so it's worth taking two Advil to read through this stuff! Here's what I want you to remember:

1. Start adding money to a retirement account *as soon as possible*. Even waiting until you're thirty years old will put you at a disadvantage compared to someone who starts right out of college.

2. If your employer offers a 401(k), contribute up to the amount they're willing to match. If they don't contribute anything or if the fees from the 401(k) are too high, open up a Roth IRA at a discount brokerage firm.

3. If you're not into trading stocks or picking out mutual funds, stick with investing in target date funds, as they put your retirement savings into autopilot mode.

4. Make this process easy by automating your retirement savings. If you have a 401(k), ask your HR department to automatically contribute part of your paycheck to it. If you have a Roth IRA, talk to your discount brokerage firm and ask it to link it to your checking account so at least 10 percent of your annual income gets automatically added to your Roth IRA.

11

NOW WHAT?
YOUR ACTION PLAN

It's been a blast taking you on this financial journey. But I don't want to write up a bunch of facts, tips, and statistics and then just say good-bye. So here's a ten-step plan for action you should take after reading this book. It's one thing to read a financial book and be flooded with advice, but it's another to actually act on the information and use it to change your life for the better—and that's what I want you to do!

1. Expense Tracking: You need to keep a budget if you ever want to get a true sense of your financial standing. Trying to change your monetary situation without knowing how much you spend and how much you save is like trying to lose weight without ever stepping on a scale. So to get your finances in order, start tracking every penny you save. It sounds tedious—and it is—but when your money is messy, there's only one thing to do: clean it up. Whether you use the spreadsheets we talked about; the expense calculator on my site, HelpSaveMyDollars.com; or smartphone apps, it doesn't matter—just get it done!

2. Automate Your Savings: Remember we talked about how you can have a certain amount of money transferred from your checking account and into your savings account each month? Well, do it! It takes about two minutes to set this up on your bank's website. This way, you can save money with your eyes closed and make do with less money. Take a break from reading this list and log on to your account to make this happen now. That means now! Go!

3. Start *Actually* Saving Money: Save money by paying less for the things you buy. And how do you do that? Well, start gathering those coupons. If you know you're about to make a rather large purchase at a specific store, get on the Internet to see if you can buy a gift card to that store for a discounted price.

4. Build Up Some Credit History: The way to do this is by getting a credit card. If you're reading this now and don't have your own credit card, what are you waiting for? Simply go to a credit card company's website and apply for one! If you get rejected, then get a secured credit card, where you actually provide the card's credit limit. Once you get the card, remember that it's only to be used for small purchases, and not as a way to finance a fancier lifestyle.

5. Smash Your Debt: Have you had a bad experience with a credit card and found yourself drowning in thousands of dollars of debt? Big deal! There are plenty of strategies you can use to dig yourself out of the hole. Right now, do a quick Google search for "no-fee balance transfer cards," so you can transfer your debt (which is probably on a high-interest credit card costing you money) to a balance transfer card with a zero percent rate for at least a year, sometimes eighteen months. And if you have debt on more than one credit card, start paying off the card with the highest interest rate first, since it is the one costing you the most money. Once that card is paid off, focus on the card with the second-highest balance, and keep this process up until all your cards are paid off.

6. Pay Your Bills on Time: Credit card bills are due on the same date each month, so set a reminder on your smartphone's calendar to ping you three days beforehand. Remember, 35 percent of your FICO score is based on whether or not you pay your bills on time. The rest of your bills should be paid on time too (just sayin').

7. Student Loans: When applying for college or grad school, fill out that FAFSA form to see how much federal aid you can get. If you don't get enough federal aid to cover the cost of your tuition, then think about private student loans, which, again, are only a last resort.

8. Landing That Job or Internship: After you finish the next couple of pages of this book, flip back to where we talked about résumé writing and make sure you update your résumé accordingly. Get in touch with your school's career services department. Create a list of companies that you'd like to intern with or work at in the future. These organizations need talented people, and you're one of them. So go get 'em!

9. Retirement: Please, please, and please open up a Roth IRA at this very moment.

> That's right. Stop reading and open up a Roth IRA right now, online, at a discount brokerage firm. It takes less than ten minutes.

> I'm going to assume you just opened up the Roth IRA. Good, because the first step is to start putting money in it. You can add up to $5,000 to the account each year. So start putting $50–$100 a month into the account—whatever you can afford. Select a target date fund to invest it in, from the brokerage firm where you opened the account. That way you don't have to manage your retirement investments. That's the goal of target date funds—to make life easy.

10. Believe! This is the most important part of the book. If you don't believe in yourself, financial, career, or life success won't happen. I want you to only think positively. I don't even want the thought of not having a job to cross your mind. Only focus on the good things. And let me tell you, if you are stuck—if you feel like no one is listening—turn your life around. Picture your dream life, whether it's a dream job, a dream spouse, or $10 million in the bank. Make those goals a part of who you are. Then I want you to change your computer's desktop background to a picture of something you want in life. Maybe it's a vacation home, a new car, a specific job, or a picture of a letter saying all your student loans have been paid off. This way, every time you log on to your computer, you'll be reminded of your goals and stay focused on them.

And if I can leave you with one piece of advice on the topic of goals and success, it's this: never let any one tell you you can't do something. *Never*. Hey, I was told I couldn't take AP English in high school, and look—I ended up writing a book! So set your sights high and put yourself out there. And if you want to share your success story with me, feel free to visit my site and send me an e-mail (it's Scott@HelpSave-MyDollars.com, by the way!). And while you're at it, let me know what you think about the book by following me on Twitter@ScottGamm (also @SaveMyDollars) and Facebook .com/HelpSaveMyDollars.

Thanks for reading!

Scott

Acknowledgments

I will always be grateful for those who helped make the writing of this book possible—and there were many!

First, thanks to my family: my incredible parents, Donna Gamm and Harvey Gamm, who are always there for me and inspire me! My two older sisters—Shari and Lindsay—words will never express how much I love you. And their husbands, James Guardino and Mike Syzmanski, you guys are the best! And my grandparents, Louise and Gus Eschbacher, and my late grandparents, Freda and Irving Gamm.

I want to thank the incredible team at Penguin's Plume imprint. Kate Napolitano, my editor, was not only a lot of fun to work with, but her ideas, passion and expertise were overwhelming—and I am so grateful, Kate. Thank you for your tireless work!

Also at Plume, Phil Budnick, Elizabeth Keenan and Nadia Kashper—thanks for the opportunity of a lifetime to write this book.

And the book would not have been possible had it not

been for my supersmart literary agent, Jesseca Salky of Hannigan Salky Getzler Agency. Jesseca, thank you for looking out for me and for answering the many, many questions I always have!

I'd also like to thank the following members of the media who have been so generous and helpful: Debbie Kosofsky, Cecilia Fang, Tammy Filler, Ann Curry, Kathie Lee Gifford, Jonathan San, Dan Holway, Linda Wolf, Matt Pitzer, Angie Dorr, Contessa Brewer, Alex Witt, Darlene Rodriguez, Shiba Russell, David Ushery, Enez Paganuzi, Sharon Raifer, Ryan Ruggiero, Andrew Ross Sorkin, Brian Shactman, Bob Psani, Nik Deogun, Mandy Drury, Bill Griffeth, Dorian Langlais, Allen Wastler, Deborah Caldwell, Albert Bozzo, Stephanie Landsman, Maneet Ahuja, Shartia Brantley, Karin Caifa, Erin Burnett, Tanya Rivero, Ben Sherwood, Barbara Fedida, Jeffrey Schneider, Teresa Song, Ashley Momtaheni, Santina Leuci, Brandon Bodow, Matt Frucci, Bianna Golodryga, Phil Lipof, Ojinika Obiekwe, Kate Sullivan, Marcia Parris, Sukanya Krishnan, Frances Rivera, Craig Treadway, Tamsen Fadal, Tracey Eyers, Eric Berlin, Rob Morrison, Cindy Hsu, Joe Silvestri, Tai Hernandez, Tracy Byrnes, David Asman, Kevin Magee, Sacha Janke, Kate Rogers, Emily Driscoll, Rachel Boyman, Brian Donlon, Alexis Glick, Paula Rizzo, Jordan Chariton, Christopher Snyder, Alison Taub, Ashley Diamond, Tracy Langer Chevrier, JD Roberto, Audra Lowe, Dawn Papandrea, Ondine Irving, Dave Carpenter, Matt Schifrin, Zack O'Malley Greenburg, Steve Schaefer, Tina Russo, and John Dobosz.

And a shout-out to Carmin Biggs, a producer at WABC-

TV who put me on TV at the young age of seventeen to talk about money—this was my first TV appearance back in 2009!

Also the amazing team at *TheStreet* (where I write weekly): Marc Levy, Eric Rosenbaum, and Kali Geldis. At Participant Media Television, I want to thank Evan Shapiro for his help and guidance.

And I'd like to thank these financial stars who have been so kind with their time and advice: David Bach, Beth Kobliner, Liz Weston, Lynette Khalfani-Cox, Jeff Yeager, Farnoosh Torabi, Manisha Thakor, Nicole Lapin, Andrea Woroch, and David Darst.

At NYU's Stern School of Business—thanks to Professor Barbara Holt, Dean Susan Greenbaum, and Tiffany Boselli.

I also want to thank the readers of my site, HelpSaveMyDollars.com—thanks for your passion for personal finance!

Notes

Introduction

1. http://www.consumerfinance.gov/blog/too-big-to-fail-student-debt-hits-a-trillion/
2. https://www1.salliemae.com/about/news_info/newsreleases/041309.htm
3. Ibid.
4. Ibid.
5. http://www.jumpstart.org/state-financial-educationrequirements.html

Chapter 1

1. http://www.foxbusiness.com/personal-finance/2012/05/04/pay-more-in-taxes-than-on-housing-food-and-clothing-combined/

Chapter 2

1. http://money.cnn.com/2009/12/02/news/economy/fdic_survey/
2. http://www.bloomberg.com/news/2012-03-08/wells-fargo-ends-free-checking-with-7-fee-added-in-six-more-u-s-states.html

3. http://www.unfaircreditcardfees.com/site/press/usa_today_
   article_punctures_banks_swipe_fee_myths
4. http://www.consumerreports.org/cro/consumer-reports-
   magazine-february-2012/bank-accounts/index.htm
5. http://money.usnews.com/money/personal-finance/
   articles/2011/10/21/considering-a-credit-union-3-factors-to-
   think-about
6. Ibid.
7. http://www.federalreserve.gov/paymentsystems/regii-average-
   interchange-fee.htm
8. http://www.nytimes.com/2011/06/30/business/30debit
   .html?_r=0
9. http://www.cardhub.com/edu/interchange-fee-study-2010/
10. http://moneyland.time.com/2012/05/07/swipe-fee-caps-are-
    here-so-where-are-the-savings/
11. http://www.crainsnewyork.com/article/20120420/
    FINANCE/120429997
12. http://www.moebs.com/PressReleases/tabid/58/ctl/Details/
    mid/380/ItemID/199/Default.aspx
13. http://www.pewtrusts.org/uploadedFiles/wwwpewtrustsorg/
    Fact_Sheets/Safe_Checking/Overdraft_America_Final.pdf
14. Ibid.
15. Source for all overdraft info: http://www.federalreserve.gov/
    consumerinfo/wyntk_overdraft.htm
16. http://www.ftc.gov/bcp/edu/pubs/consumer/credit/cre04
    .shtm
17. https://www.javelinstrategy.com/brochure/247 and http://
    www.mainstreet.com/article/moneyinvesting/credit/debt/
    prepaid-cards-growing-popularity
18. http://www.bankrate.com/calculators/savings/cd-laddering-
    calculator.aspx

Chapter 3

1. http://knowledge.wharton.upenn.edu/article
   .cfm?articleid=2132

2. http://www.mobilecommercedaily.com/2012/05/17/53pc-of-mobile-users-stop-an-in-store-purchase-because-of-their-phone

3. http://www.mainstreet.com/article/smart-spending/technology/email-not-social-media-largest-driver-online-purchases

4. http://newsroom.mastercard.com/press-releases/new-mastercard-advisors-study-on-contactless-payments-shows-almost-30-lift-in-total-spend-within-first-year-of-adoption/

5. http://www.prnewswire.com/news-releases/seven-in-ten-americans-cooking-more-instead-of-going-out-to-save-money-151684925.html

6. http://www.amtrak.com/servlet/ContentServer?c=Page&pagename=am%2FLayout&cid=1241305460134

7. http://www.gpo.gov/fdsys/pkg/PLAW-110publ315/html/PLAW-110publ315.htm

Chapter 4

1. http://www.forbes.com/pictures/mhj45ihgi/worst-cities-to-rent-no-1-new-york-ny/#gallerycontent

Chapter 5

1. http://moneyland.time.com/2012/05/08/why-are-credit-report-errors-so-hard-to-fix/

2. http://bucks.blogs.nytimes.com/2012/05/03/report-finds-improvement-in-credit-scores/?ref=your-money

3. http://www.myfico.com/CreditEducation/WhatsInYourScore.aspx

Chapter 6

1. http://www.foxbusiness.com/personal-finance/2012/06/06/rate-survey-credit-card-interest-rates-down-slightly/

2. http://www.reuters.com/article/2012/04/18/us-credit-cards-howmany-idUSBRE83H0U620120418

3. https://www1.salliemae.com/about/news_info/newsreleases/041309.htm

4. http://www.ftc.gov/bcp/edu/pubs/consumer/credit/cre04.shtm

5. http://www.livescience.com/2849-study-credit-cards-spending.html

6. http://www.federalreserve.gov/boarddocs/rptcongress/creditcard/2010/downloads/CCAP_October_web.pdf

7. http://www.mainstreet.com/article/moneyinvesting/credit/debt/card-act-fails-protect-students

8. http://online.wsj.com/article/SB100014240527023047244045772297860607013698.html

9. Ibid.

Chapter 7

1. https://www1.salliemae.com/about/news_info/newsreleases/041309.htm

2. http://www.federalreserve.gov/pubs/bulletin/2012/pdf/scf12.pdf

3. http://www.guardian.co.uk/money/2010/jul/21/debt-problems-impact-health

4. Tosto, Paul, "The Private Lives of College Students: From Condom Use to Credit Card Debt, Survey Charts Factors Affecting Health," *McClatchy-Tribune Business News*, November 16, 2007: http://search.proquest.com/docview/463603026

5. Adams, Troy, and Monique Moore, "High-Risk Health and Credit Behavior Among 18- to 25-Year-Old College Students," *Journal of American College Health*, vol. 56, no. 2 (2007): 101–8: http://search.proquest.com/pqcentral/docview/213087772/1376D57952B24A44D09/50?accountid=12768

Chapter 8

1. http://trends.collegeboard.org/downloads/College_
   Pricing_2011.pdf
2. http://www.washingtonpost.com/national/higher-education/
   ed-department-college-costs-rising-price-to-attend-a-4-year-
   public-university-up-15-percent/2012/06/12/gJQA2SXvXV_
   story.html
3. http://trends.collegeboard.org/downloads/College_
   Pricing_2011.pdf
4. http://studentaid.ed.gov/fafsa/filling-out/dependency
5. http://www.fafsa.ed.gov/fotw1112/pdf/PdfFafsa11-12.pdf
6. http://professionals.collegeboard.com/profdownload/
   PROFILE_fees.pdf
7. http://www.studentaid.ed.gov/types/loans/subsidized-
   unsubsidized
8. http://www.ed.gov/news/press-releases/default-rates-rise-
   federal-student-loans
9. http://studentaid.ed.gov/PORTALSWebApp/students/
   english/IBRPlan.jsp
10. http://studentaid.ed.gov/repay-loans/consolidation
11. http://bucks.blogs.nytimes.com/2012/05/07/sallie-mae-will-
    offer-fixed-rate-private-student-loans/ and https://www1
    .salliemae.com/about/news_info/newsreleases/Sallie+Mae+
    introduces+Fixed-Rate+Private+Education+Loan.htm
12. https://www.wellsfargo.com/student/consolidateloans/
    privatestudentloans

Chapter 9

1. http://mashable.com/2010/10/16/twitter-hashtags-job-search/
2. http://www.wired.com/wiredscience/2012/05/st_cuddy/
3. http://online.wsj.com/article/SB1000142405297020383300457
   7249360596365388.html

Chapter 10

1. http://www.demos.org/press-release/new-report-hidden-excessive-401k-fees-cost-retirees-155000
2. http://www.dol.gov/opa/media/press/ebsa/EBSA20111653.htm

Index